DATE DUE

			PRINTED IN U.S.A.

APR 0 1 2013

TEACHING WITH THE SCREEN

"Dan Leopard tackles some complex topics but is so comfortable in his own skin that it takes much of the anxiety out of the process. I am certain this book will be read with interest by advanced undergraduates and college-educated lay readers and the most curious of classroom educators who are seeking new ways of making sense of the impact of media change on their professional practices and on the lives of their students."

Henry Jenkins, University of Southern California

"Leopard presents an interesting account of his experience using technology to teach media culture covering a wide range of types of media that function as pedagogy. Clearly on-line and virtual teaching is an emerging trend so it is valuable to have an informed and experienced voice like his analyzing different modes of teaching with machines."

Doug Kellner, University of California at Los Angeles

Teaching with the Screen explores the forms that pedagogy takes as teachers and students engage with the screens of popular culture. By necessity, these forms of instruction challenge traditional notions of what constitutes education. Placing media-based pedagogy at the intersection of education, anthropology, and cultural studies, this book traces a path across historically specific instances of media that function as pedagogy: Hollywood films that feature teachers as protagonists, a public television course on French language and culture, a daily television "news" program created by high-school students, and a virtual reality training simulation funded by the US Army. These case studies focus on teachers as pedagogical agents (teacher plus screen) who unite the two figures that have polarized earlier debates regarding the use of media and technology in educational settings: the beloved teacher and the teaching machine.

Spotlighting the visual, spatial, and relational aspects of media-based pedagogy using a broad range of critical methodologies—textual analysis, interviews, and participant observation—this rich narrative and analytical mosaic of ethnographic research embedded within an engaging historical framework provides a strong conceptual model of media-based pedagogy with which to understand the uses of media in education over the past fifty years.

Dan Leopard is Associate Professor of Media and Cultural Studies at Saint Mary's College in the San Francisco Bay Area, USA.

TEACHING WITH THE SCREEN

PEDAGOGY, AGENCY, AND MEDIA CULTURE

Dan Leopard
SAINT MARY'S COLLEGE OF CALIFORNIA

 Routledge
Taylor & Francis Group

NEW YORK AND LONDON

First published 2013
by Routledge
711 Third Avenue, New York, NY 10017

Simultaneously published in the UK
by Routledge
2 Park Square, Milton Park, Abingdon, Oxon OX14 4RN

Routledge is an imprint of the Taylor & Francis Group, an informa business

Library of Congress Cataloging in Publication Data
Leopard, Dan, 1959–
    Teaching with the screen : pedagogy, agency, and media culture / Dan
    Leopard.
    p. cm.
    Includes bibliographical references and index.
    1. Motion pictures in education. 2. Audio-visual education. 3. Mass media in
    education. 4. Educational films. I. Title.
    LB1044.L47 2012
    371.33'523—dc23
    2012030133

ISBN: 978-0-415-64062-6(hbk)
ISBN: 978-0-203-08264-5(ebk)

Typeset in Bembo and Stone Sans
by EvS Communication Networx, Inc.

To Jen and Jer. And to all of the other futures.

CONTENTS

PREFACE

The practice of pedagogy changes to suit new or renewed conditions of the classroom as teachers and students engage with popular culture in the form of screen media and technologies. By necessity, these transformations of pedagogical practice challenge, and to a great extent undermine, traditional notions of what the structure and content of education should be. To many of those teachers and administrators with the greatest stake in the educational status quo, these changes can be perceived as threatening and therefore need to be either co-opted or nullified. To others with an interest in educational innovation these same changes can be seen as a blissful frenzy of revolutionary ideas and barrier-breaking educational techniques that need to be proselytized to the masses of fellow teachers, students, and administrators. In this book, I seek a descriptive and analytical middle distance where the changes that have occurred in the pedagogical uses of media and technology can be seen as a part of the larger history of the transformation of schooling, formal and informal, over the past fifty years.

Consequently, *Teaching with the Screen* traces a path across historically specific instances of screen-based media that function as pedagogy: Hollywood films that feature teachers as protagonists; a well-known public television course on French language and culture; a daily television "news" program produced by high school students; and a virtual reality training simulation housed at a major research university and funded by the U.S. Army. These case studies focus on teachers as pedagogical agents who unite the two figures that have polarized earlier debates around schools, students, and public policy regarding the use of media in educational settings: the beloved teacher and the teaching machine.

The wistful, nostalgic figure of the beloved teacher, drawn as it is from memories of one's youth, summons up for many people what is most admirable about education. The beloved teacher is well-represented by the character of the befuddled yet warmly supportive headmaster Mr. Chipping (ably portrayed with nostalgic aplomb by Robert Donat in the 1939 film *Goodbye Mr. Chips*). In contrast, the teaching machine represents, especially to those former students subjected to the worst that educational technology has to offer, teaching as an assembly line of "programmed instruction" evoking the dystopias of numerous science fiction scenarios (easily calling to mind the iconic malevolence of the Hal 9000 computer in Stanley Kubrick's 1968 film *2001: A Space Odyssey*). Both of these figures of the teacher, the beloved and the machine, in large part bracket the historical public discourse on the uses of media and technology in education.

But, a figure of more recent conception, the "pedagogical agent"—deployed as a metaphorical figure derived from research agendas in cognitive science and artificial intelligence—suggests other ways of understanding pedagogy as it plays across the screens of film, television, video, and digital media. The pedagogical agent, at once a machine and a representation of the beloved flesh-and-blood teacher, opens up the possibility for the creation of future "teaching machines" that bear the affective qualities most of us would mark as deeply human: programmed for instruction, yet emotionally and cognitively complex. This form of virtual human, designed to provide simultaneously efficient and humanistic teaching, serves as the key conceptual figure through which this book examines the interplay between pedagogy, agency, and media culture.

Thus, *Teaching with the Screen* weaves an argument through a series of critical, ethnographically informed analyses of pedagogical agents—cinematic teachers, media students, TV professors, and virtual humans. These pedagogical agents and their teaching practices are examined in relation to a transdisciplinary theoretical framework drawn from education, ethnography, and media and cultural studies. Educational theory helps the reader to place the actions of the agents in the context of the traditions of teaching and learning, ethnography helps to frame these practices within the larger institutional contexts in which they are embedded, and media and cultural studies enable one to understand the relationship that exists between the texts, practices, and popular culture. Each media text discussed at length in the book signals the creation of a form of agency that centers on an interaction between teacher and student so that a variety of screens work to "present," "augment," or "embody" the teacher in the representational medium that he or she inhabits.

With this emphasis on screens and teachers, this study therefore focuses on the visual, spatial, and relational aspects of media-based pedagogy using a broad range of critical methodologies: textual analysis, interviews, and participant observation. This mixed methods approach to the subject should provide a strong conceptual model (an archaeological model to use Foucault's terminology) with which to understand the uses of media in education over the past fifty years. This is in contrast to much of the existing research on media education (especially in the area of new media) which seems to display a petite form of social and cultural amnesia by taking a resolutely presentist stance that forgets the longstanding relationship between media technologies and educational practice. That history is what structures this book and I hope will deepen the reader's understanding of what is different about today's attempts at media pedagogy and what remains similar. While the book focuses on the U.S. educational context, it foregrounds the generalizable contours of media and education and thus should have relevance to those teachers and students who participate in educational discourse in a global context (for sure in the UK, Australia, and Europe, but perhaps further afield as well).

Structure

Teaching with the Screen begins with a brief sketch of my high school art teacher, Mr. Tamberlin. By summoning forth this figure from my past, I attempt to capture the teacher–student relationship that so often sets the terms for understanding pedagogy. Mr. Tamberlin, through his odd blend of conventional art instruction and cinematic curatorial practice, undermines simplistic notions of the anecdotal yet evocative nature of the beloved teacher found in media representing schooling. The remainder of the introduction focuses on the methodological background to the case studies featured throughout the book.

Chapter 1 opens on Glenn Ford's Richard Dadier crossing a busy street in the Bronx to step into the "blackboard jungle" of 1950s American public education. *Blackboard Jungle*—an exemplar of the social problem films that feature teachers using innovative pedagogy as a solution to juvenile delinquency and failing schools—becomes the template for understanding the narrative tropes of otherness and authenticity that appear in cinematic accounts of teachers and written accounts of ethnographers. These tropes, organized as they are around "arrival scenes" and "pedagogical breakthroughs," demarcate the narrative forms that structure the agency of both teachers and ethnographers.

Chapter 2 surveys the history of interactions between pedagogical agents and the screens of education: blackboard, 16 mm film, television, video, and computer. These screens are surfaces through which pedagogical agency flows through teachers (rightly the conduits of pedagogy to the public), their students (positioned by popular culture as resistant to schooling), and educational media (represented as "boring," "inspirational," or "time-killers," but rarely as strictly pedagogical). Grounded in notions of power and agency derived from media and cultural theory, pedagogical agents and their screens produce three distinct modes of instruction: the teacher presented, the teacher augmented, and the teacher embodied.

Chapter 3 looks at Professor Pierre Capretz and his PBS telecourse *French in Action* as a significant contribution to pedagogical agency presented by the television screen. In the 1960s, Capretz, language instructor and amateur cinema auteur, created multimedia lectures incorporating film clips from French New Wave cinema. These lectures developed a presentational style that eventually became his 1987 telecourse. Capretz constructs French film and media as exemplars of "Frenchness" and France as a location of tourist spectacle. The chapter concludes with observational data illustrating the ways in which *French in Action* is used as a pedagogical text at Yale University.

Chapter 4 examines *Trauber TV*, a news program produced by California high school students, as pedagogical agency augmented by screen technologies. Augmentation redefines pedagogical agency by more evenly distributing power across teachers, students, and media. Episodes of *Trauber TV* featured, at various times, mashups of drag performances, talk shows, and a steel cage death match à la the World Wrestling Federation. These representations challenged the power that held fast at the high school and in a local community defined by a minority white power structure that had dominated the larger Latino culture of the city for decades.

Chapter 5 traces the development of the STEVE virtual human simulation as pedagogical agency embodied within interactive media. Steve was designed to train U.S. army officers for combat in field settings throughout the world. In much the same way that cognition and speech are programmed into other kinds of artificial intelligence systems, Steve is also programmed for affect—politeness, anger, or respect—depending on the needs of the simulation scenario. Therefore, the chapter is organized around the otherness of machines and a semiotics of affect as demonstrated by an ethnographically informed analysis of several troubleshooting sessions carried out at the Institute for Creative Technologies, the organization of cognitive scientists and designers behind Steve.

A short concluding chapter looks at the ongoing debate between those who believe that presence—the physical sensation of the human body, here and now—is what determines the quality of interaction between teacher and student and those who suggest that mediated forms of communication can simulate, with sufficient verisimilitude, the affective and intellectual bond associated with the beloved teacher. The book concludes by suggesting that the production of pedagogy by agents and machines must not be allowed to overshadow pedagogy as a form of gift between two subjectivities: human and human, or human and machine.

ACKNOWLEDGMENTS

Central to this project are the teachers who have exerted significant influence on my life and thought. Less obviously, those I have known in other capacities as friends, allies, or adversaries have also left their pedagogical mark. As I emphasize throughout this book, pedagogy extends beyond the classroom and manifests itself in ways that often go unrecognized or, worse yet, simply ignored.

Obviously, those who have taught me most recently have had the greatest influence on the intellectual contours of this project. In this regard, many thanks to Michael Renov, David E. James, Marsha Kinder, and Tara McPherson from the University of Southern California's School of Cinematic Arts for their expert guidance on all things related to screens (documentary and avant-garde), media technologies (new, old, and interactive), critical theory, and cultural studies while I completed the dissertation that resides at the heart of this book. Special thanks to William G. Tierney from USC's Rossier School of Education for his patience in guiding me through issues pertaining to qualitative research and curriculum and instruction. In addition, while studying at USC I had the good fortune to work with a distinguished group of scholars and teachers who contributed to my thinking and research while I was working on my doctorate: Dana Polan, Lynn Spigel, Jeff Sconce, Doe Mayer, Don Miller, Selma Holo, Max Schulz, and Bill Whittington: Many thanks to you as well.

Extending back in time and across miles of geography, I also wish to acknowledge the debt I hold to the many teachers who served as models of what great pedagogy could be: Don Richardson, Tom Veatch, John Conway, Sharon Bronzan, Allison Renwick, Walton Fosque, Jim Kitses, Robert Bell, Trinh T. Minh-ha, Ellen Zweig, Christine Tamblyn, Lynn Hershman, Steve Fagin, Donald Lowe, Sheila Meneely, John Manning, Lin Hixson, Margaret

Olin, Judith Kirschner, Peter Taub, Lorraine McLeod, and Mark Phillips. Each of you has contributed something essential.

As for the research itself, thanks are in order to those who provided their time and expertise as I carried out my research: The faculty, students, and administrators of John Trauber High School in Vista Valley, California; Professor Pierre Capretz and the faculty of the Yale University French Department; and the researchers and staff at the Institute for Creative Technologies and the Information Sciences Institute at USC. I hope that I have not treated indiscriminately what you gave so freely. And thank you to Professors Larry Cuban and Henry Jenkins for their intellectual generosity and support at various points in the development of the project. At Routledge, thanks to Naomi Silverman and Julie Ganz for their steady encouragement while guiding this book through the editorial process.

Thanks are also due to those colleagues in academia who have been helpful in ways that they may not even begin to fathom: Noah Shenker, Heidi Rae Cooley, Deepak Sawhney, Peter Freund, Ellen Rigsby, Scott Rustin, Karen Beavers, Stephanie DeBoer, Karen Bowdre, Miae Choi, Michele Lowry, Steve Anderson, Holly Willis, and Rich Edwards; Mike and Valerie for helping me make it through the credential program ("You know, kids these days read *Oedipus Rex* in the morning and *Sweet Valley High* in the evening."); Dave and Marilyn Forrest, Susan Speakman, and Rhonda Neagle at the New Haven Unified School District; the Sydney Circle, those from Ghent University, and my comrades in the Communication Department at Saint Mary's College of California.

Finally, thanks to Steve, Darryl, Judie and Mick, Melvin and Dorothy, Emy and John, and, of course, Dawnalyn.

INTRODUCTION

Studying Media in Educational Settings

Reality is a construction. Certainly life must be observed for it to appear.
Yet it is by no means contained in the more or less random observational
results of reportage; rather it is to be found solely in the mosaic that is
assembled from single observations on the basis of comprehension of their
meaning. Reportage photographs life; such a mosaic would be its image.

—Siegfried Kracauer, *The Salaried Masses*[1]

Film Fridays with Mr. Tamberlin

Mr. Tamberlin, the art teacher at Burroughs Polytechnic High School, screened
16 mm films most Fridays throughout the year. His screenings were an eclectic
set of short art and instructional films presumably ordered from the Mult-
nomah County Office of Education's audiovisual department. On any given
Friday, Mr. Tamberlin's film program might consist of a 1950s film about agri-
culture in Oregon's Hood River Valley, a quasi-surrealist film produced by the
National Film Board of Canada, and possibly a condensation of a Hollywood
theatrical film such as *A Tale of Two Cities* starring Ronald Coleman. Since art
class followed lunch, which often was spent outside in the dreary gray rain, Mr.
Tamberlin's screenings served as refuge from the bleak weather and the overall
sense of gray that set upon Portland, Oregon in the mid-1970s. Mr. Tamberlin's choice of films to screen—quirky, trashy, and marvelous—transported his
students (well, at least me) to artistic worlds little known through viewings of
nightly network television or screenings of Hollywood double features at the
Montavilla Theater, a second-run movie house in our neighborhood.

Mr. Tamberlin was a flamboyant man. Most days he wore thrift store clothing: a fluffy white buccaneer shirt accompanied by black wool marching band

pants and saddle shoes. His unkempt mane of hair was shoulder length, a sure sign of counterculture affiliation in those days, and was greased back, giving him the look of a slightly demented orchestra conductor. He often came to class with several days' worth of beard stubble. His classroom was filled with black lights, psychedelic posters (apparently purchased from local head shops), and the clutter of art production—drawing tablets, dried paint cans, tubs of camel hair brushes, and half-finished student art projects. Music of every sort played incessantly over Mr. Tamberlin's paint splattered transistor radio or on the school-issued all-in-one phonograph that he kept in his room. On some days we sketched to top forty pop songs, on others we printed silkscreen t-shirts to bebop jazz.

The clutch of students who hung around his room during lunchtime and after school had a slightly "stoner" art nerd aura about them. These were the same kids who could be seen smoking cigarettes and "doobies" at the "round house," the campus maintenance building, every morning before school. Although administrators constantly warned us, the "good kids," that hanging out and smoking before school could earn us several days worth of detention, these "bad kids" could be seen at the round house every morning without fail. This open flaunting of school rules lent these students a mystique that carried over into Mr. Tamberlin's room. They were usually assigned to instruct the students new to the class on how to accomplish some specific art technique or how to handle some equipment during a complex production process. These teaching assistants followed through with their assigned tasks with an air of aloofness that at once thrilled and frightened the young art neophyte. And overseeing all of these students with an even greater sense of elevated detachment was Mr. Tamberlin.

His Friday film series acquired an air of countercultural hipness as much from the screening space—a darkened classroom outfitted with psychedelic posters and hippie décor—as from the consecration as a form of art (with a capital "A," in this instance) given to the films through association with Mr. Tamberlin.[2] If Mr. Tamberlin thought these movies were worth watching there must be something more to them than just a random assortment of styles and topics. I often felt confused and uncertain as to what I had seen on film Fridays, but I usually assumed that there must have been some merit to each film screened. As the year wore on, many of the films seemed to be afterthoughts, as if the county's media catalog had already offered up its treasures and now we were watching the leftovers, but occasionally a transcendentally brilliant and weird film would appear, and the whole process would be reinvigorated. Several times films that I had seen in elementary school were screened (such as *The Loon's Necklace* (1949), which retold a North Coast Indian myth by representing the main characters with Native American masks), and the changed context would allow me to see the film in a renewed way.

In the several years that followed, I remembered Mr. Tamberlin's screenings and his use of these films as not much more than an entertaining and slightly bizarre diversion from more traditionally rigorous approaches to art instruction. Eventually, I forgot about Mr. Tamberlin and his Friday film series altogether.

Pedagogy and Media Production

As an adult, I found myself teaching television production at John Trauber High School in the San Francisco Bay Area. The teacher who preceded me had quit over disagreements with the school's administration of his program, so consequently I was left with a skeletal curriculum and little guidance as to how to structure my course. I found myself "winging" early classes, basing most of my instruction on several courses I had taught at local community colleges. As anyone who has taught at both high school and community college knows, the student population and the school resources are often quite different. High school students are demanding, by virtue of compulsory education, in ways that college students, who elect to attend class, rarely are. My attempts at teaching in a media-saturated educational environment—too many students, too much damaged equipment, and not enough time to prepare for classes—proved to be ineffective. I found myself searching for a pedagogical approach that would work with these particular students in this particular educational setting.

After several months of trial and error I eventually settled upon a form of teaching practice that for the most part worked with a curriculum that needed to be equal parts instruction *and* production. The specifics of my teaching practice and how it transformed my relations with students and the larger school community will be examined in detail in chapter 4, but here I want to acknowledge that upon reflection much of my pedagogical method was modeled on my latent memories of Mr. Tamberlin. Of course, there were aspects to my teaching that I gathered from other teachers at other times, but the core of my teaching practice came by way of Mr. Tamberlin. As has been suggested by sociological studies of education, modeling teaching practice after that of a beloved teacher is one powerful way that teaching techniques are transmitted from one generation of teachers to another, even if one fails to recognize how much this influence matters.[3]

At the time, Mr. Tamberlin most likely thought of me as a quiet, artistically inclined student who responded awkwardly when spoken to and generally avoided interactions with other students. For most of the class I would bury my nose in my drawing pad and contentedly scribble away. Obviously, on Fridays the film screenings gave me an even greater anonymity while I worked on my sketches. Over time, I am sure that Mr. Tamberlin forgot my name and possibly even my obsessive drawing technique, but, regardless, his feel for teaching, eccentric ways, cadre of loyal art groupies, and careful attention to even the most shy of first year students (conveyed through instruction provided with warmth and good humor) had in some manner structured my conception, at a deeply cognitive and affective level, of what constituted "good" teaching. And years later, mired in the educational fog of my first year teaching in a public school, I flailed around for instructional technique and found these ghosts of Mr. Tamberlin inhabiting my unconscious.

But the influence that Mr. Tamberlin had on my teaching practice also summons up another important relationship that draws on media as much as it does memory. By setting up a projector and screening films every Friday, Mr. Tamberlin set up the preconditions for students to perceive media, in this case film, as an exemplary form of visual instruction and artistic inspiration (in addition to being an entertaining release from the often rigid institutional strictures of education and work). Through these screenings, and the foundation they provided for his curriculum, he encouraged his students to broaden their worldview and to become excited about subjects that jumped the boundaries of traditional visual arts instruction. By using media in this way, he "spoke" to his students in a language that reflected the interests and concerns of their daily lives.

The stoner round house kids were drawn to Mr. Tamberlin because of the whiff of counterculture that hovered around him (a counterculture that was itself constructed through and by the media) and because he accepted the message that these students were offering with their long hair and unkempt appearance. He was one of them, but experienced and knowledgeable in art and life in ways that legitimated his approach to teaching. With the films (and perhaps the ubiquitous black lights and posters) he opened up the possibility for transformed perception by questioning, even if imperfectly, what had become conventional in education, and through his capacity as an elective teacher, always a minority role in public schools, he allowed students to push the boundaries of what was possible culturally, socially, and academically throughout the school.[4] Film Fridays fit with his approach to instruction and his classroom demeanor as exhibited on a daily basis. Through his wit and insight, his intense visual presence, his emphasis on creating an educational community, and his reliance on media and art as fundamental forms of instruction, Mr. Tamberlin remains for me an exemplary teacher. And as my own instance of the beloved teacher, a figure to be examined in some detail, he will linger over the research that follows.

A Reading of Readings

The research methodology used throughout *Teaching with the Screen* draws upon work from audience studies (derived from media and cultural studies) and media ethnography (derived from anthropology and documentary studies). Audience studies and media ethnography have generated complementary research agendas developing out of the ongoing dialogue between those scholars who practice textual analysis in the humanities and those who practice qualitative research in the interpretative social sciences.[5] This dialogue is the starting point for the research—observation as text and narrative as analysis—contained in *Teaching with the Screen*.

I do not want to rehash a much chronicled history, but it seems crucial that the intellectual foundations of this study be remarked upon. Unlike much of the research conducted in the name of film studies (in particular those forms developing out of 1970s "screen theory"),[6] research in audience studies has shifted the focus from the production of media (with an emphasis on the creation of texts by media industry auteurs and the effects, artistic and psychological, that these texts have on audiences) to the consumption of media (the use of media texts by specific audiences).[7] This current iteration of audience studies began as a subfield of the cross-disciplinary work being carried out in England at the University of Birmingham's Center for Contemporary Cultural Studies.[8] As such, scholars at the center took as their specific object of study audiences from the working class, a perspective consistent with their disciplinary investments in Marxism and sociology. This "studying down" as it were, focusing on subcultural groups in contrast to dominant ruling elites, was also consistent with the inspiration that those at Birmingham drew from ethnographic work conducted during the 1930s by the Chicago School of urban sociology centered at the University of Chicago.[9]

Of the many projects growing out of this period of cultural studies, David Morley's work has been particularly influential. His books *The Nationwide Television Studies,* coauthored with Charlotte Brunsdon, and *Family Television* are formative to subsequent work that focuses on the uses of television by viewers.[10] While *The Nationwide Television Studies* emphasizes a more textually centered approach, albeit still eschewing the abstraction inherent in screen theory, *Family Television* uses an ethnographic approach—focused interviews, really—to examine how people watch television and the ways that forms of watching structure relationships within the family. Morley describes his method in *Family Television* as follows:

> Eighteen families were interviewed in their own homes during the spring of 1985. Initially the two parents were interviewed, then later in each interview their children were invited to take part in the discussion along with their parents. The interviews, which lasted between one and two hours, were tape-recorded and then transcribed in full for analysis.[11]

Because he focused on a small number of families and interviewed them for short durations, Morley's work has been criticized for failing to meet the traditional requirements of ethnography, which are most often defined as field study that immerses a researcher in a specific culture for a time lasting from several months to a year or more.[12] Defending his process, Morley explains his underlying rationale for the limited scale of his studies, specifically the research for *Family Television*, as predicated on limited resources but as still superior to the paradigm of the abstract spectator that dominated film studies during its screen theory phase.[13] Morley states:

> In my own research, I have offered the reader a "reading" of the texts supplied by my respondents—those texts themselves being the respondents' accounts of their own viewing behaviour. However, in relation to the problems of the status of any knowledge that might be produced as a result of this process of "readings of readings," I would still argue that the interview (not to mention other techniques such as participant observation) remains a fundamentally more appropriate way to attempt to understand what audiences do when they watch television than for the analyst simply to stay at home and imagine the possible implications of how other people might watch television.[14]

While it can be argued that the short durations of Morley's work open up the possibility that the armchair anthropologist is just as viable as the focused interviewer, it is important that his work be seen as a critical response to the dominance of the spectatorial gaze in film studies. Empirical work on actual audiences can document the ways that cultural and media products are used in daily life, ways of action that can be obscured by the social standing and cultural assumptions that textually based media theorists often bring to their studies. In addition, drawing upon implications from the work of semiotics and structuralism, Morley also argues for a finer set of critical and empirical distinctions growing out of a "reading of readings," an interpretive strategy based on the work of viewers in response to given media and mediated environments. This reading of readings complements the procedurally based dicta of traditional definitions of what constitutes ethnographic fieldwork. Morley's work brings into media studies not just the procedures associated with sociological and anthropological fieldwork, but more importantly (certainly for this book and its research in educational settings) it introduces a mind-set, a frame of reference, which can be characterized as ethnographic. The ethnographic mind-set brings to bear on media research the problematics that have dominated theoretical discussions in the interpretative social sciences over the past thirty or so years—most importantly, those issues pertaining to the relationship between agency and structure and between subject and researcher.[15]

Morley also addresses criticism of his "ethnographic" work by media studies scholars who argue using a model of analysis dependent on political economy. Morley states that these scholars fail "to see that macro-structures can only be reproduced through micro-processes."[16] By contrasting micro-processes with macro-structures Morley provides a distinction (and a link) between the two levels of analysis that are applied to cultural forms most often by media researchers (whether they adhere to political economy or anthropology). It is the emphasis on the interactions that exist between the macro-structures (which are bound to historical processes of change and cultural/social development) and the micro-processes (which aggregate to form and are codependently determined by the macrostructures) that define Morley's use of ethnographic methods.

The long-form ethnography (which is the primary method of anthropology), often months to years in length, provides for an accumulation of observations of microprocesses, research snapshots, which can then be organized within an analytical framework that allows for explanatory statements regarding the macro-structure called culture—"a whole way of life" in the anthropological sense, as defined by Raymond Williams.[17] The long duration of traditional ethnography does provide certain procedural safeguards against research conclusions unsupported by empirical evidence (and reached through casual observation), but a less lengthy research process—a short, but rigorous observation—could conceivably provide, in Morley's terms, sufficient research evidence for a detailed analysis of a micro-object (not the presumptive object of anthropology, "culture," but a more modest account of a cultural object or setting in its partiality). Using this approach to juxtaposing the methodologies of anthropology and audience studies, the long-form ethnography suggests a feature film while the short form suggests a snapshot—an empirical slice through the temporal substance of daily life and media use.

For the ethnographically informed research presented in this study, the micro-objects, media-based pedagogies, are examined through an extensive set of fieldwork material that offers the reader a mixed set of procedural conditions. The core research material, the participant observation associated with my work as a teacher in a public secondary school, easily meets the procedural criteria for long-form ethnography as broadly described in anthropological fieldwork.[18] The other material develops out of shorter site visits that align more closely to Morley's research procedures (and are akin to a set of snapshots of texts and practices). The ethnographic mind-set that Morley employs in his work favors critical practice and empirical evidence over routine procedure and abstract universalism and thus allows for questions of agency to come into play while remaining cognizant of the structures that constrain and mark social and pedagogical interactions.

Toward Media Ethnography

Marie Gillespie's ethnographic study of British Pakistani youth as media users builds on Morley's research around gender to include questions concerning ethnicity and provides the second touchstone for the material presented in this book. As a key work of audience studies, Gillespie's *Television, Ethnicity and Cultural Change* easily meets the durational standard set for conventional ethnography (in contrast to the bulk of audience studies work that seeks inspiration from Morley).[19] She culls her research from two years spent working in a school in the Southall area of London. She uses this extensive "fieldwork" experience as the basis for an ethnographic study that delves deeply into the identity formations that are generated by her young informants as they consume television programs and popular music with their peers and families. Gillespie's interweaving of generational and ethnic identity creates for the reader a complex evocation and examination of the tensions that existed during the 1990s in Southall between the "traditional" culture of the parents at home (derived from the familiar culture of the "home" country, Pakistan) and what is perceived as the "alien" Western culture that dominated life in the UK. Her use of ethnicity and identity as a method to reframe analysis through a dialectic of other and same, home and away grounds the work in media ethnography upon which Gillespie draws for her study. Media ethnography, an at-the-time emerging subfield of anthropology, focuses on the uses of media, as production and consumption, by members of a particular culture or subculture. Gillespie, in fact, aligns herself with this disciplinary perspective at the outset and thus seeks to incorporate more strictly anthropological concerns within a revised notion of what constitutes British Cultural Studies:

> Hitherto the preserve of social anthropologists, ethnography is the empirical description and analysis of cultures based on intensive and extensive fieldwork in a selected local setting. It has much to contribute to the study of both diaspora and media cultures, and thereby to key theoretical debates in social, cultural and media studies, especially those concerning ethnicity and identity in the context of recent trends towards the simultaneous "globalization" and "localization" of culture.[20]

Here Gillespie explicitly situates her work as standing outside of the normalized trajectory of audience studies in the cultural studies vein and moves her work toward media ethnography. To date, ethnography, as the distinctive method of social and cultural anthropologists, has been effectively appropriated, often more as a metaphor than as a practice, by those in media and cultural studies as much for, as Gillespie states above, "contribut[ing] to the study of ... media cultures" as it has for its generalized framework for viewing the experience of daily life (of which media is a major component). But it is important to distinguish between an appropriation of ethnography simply as a metaphor, which some of the qualitative work labeled "postmodernist" does, and its use as an empirical framework from which to engage participants in their worlds (as alluded to in the negative by Morley in his reference to those who sit in chairs and imagine what audiences do).

While the work described above comes out of a cultural studies perspective, media ethnography is predicated on an explicitly anthropological frame of reference. Here the act of "studying down" of the Chicago School is transformed into one in which the object of study is non-Western people (the conceptualized Other of traditional anthropology) and their use of media in a global context. Much of the work in media ethnography (also called the anthropology of media) has grown out of the critique, over the past thirty years, of the colonially defined power relations out of which cultural anthropology developed. In addition, media ethnography owes much of its practical and theoretical interests not only to the work of the linguistic and visual turns in anthropology, but also to the above cited cultural studies work. By assigning agency to those studied, media ethnographers position non-Western people as using and producing media rather than simply being dominated by Western media (the cultural imperialism model) as suggested by communication scholars who study the pernicious effects of globalization and consumer culture.[21]

While audience studies research has focused on the relations between viewers and mainstream television, media ethnography focuses on local media producers and viewers in a global context. Media anthropologists Faye Ginsburg, Lila Abu-Lughod, and Brian Larkin have articulated the research goals of media ethnography as:

> [Expanding on] "what counts" in a variety of ways. Anthropologists, for example, track the social players involved when one "follows the thing"—a film or television serial as it moves from elite directors to consumers or an object like a cassette recorder, a radio, or even radio sound itself as it circulates through various milieux. Such strategies help us see not only how media are embedded in people's quotidian lives but also how consumers and producers are themselves imbricated in discursive universes, political situations, economic circumstances, national settings, historical moments, and transnational flows.[22]

These two attributes of ethnographic approaches to media, tracking indigenous uses of media and situating local media in larger regional and global contexts, constitute the research interests that inform this study. On the one hand, *Teaching with the Screen*, following the work done by Morley and others in audience studies, focuses on the uses of media and technology imbricated in educational settings, while on the other it suggests that the specific identities that are produced as a result of these practices, the forms of agency that grow out of media pedagogies, say something about the larger global mediascapes (to use Appadurai's term)[23] that dominate smaller format mediated communication (in distinct contrast to large scale mediated communication such as Hollywood movies and the corporate Internet). Consequently, *Teaching with the Screen* seeks a cross-comparative analysis of a variety of screen-based media (film, television, video, and computer simulations)[24] across a variety of educational contexts (secondary school, Ivy League university, public television, and military training). The conceptual spine of the research follows an expanded notion of teaching as a communicative and relational form of agency that is embodied by the pedagogical agents featured in the narratives that follow.

But the spirit of this study derives not only from the canon of audience studies and recent forays into media ethnography, but also from an application of a more subversive side of anthropology, the wild ethnography that developed out of the mutual interests of the surrealists and the ethnographers inhabiting Paris in the 1930s—Claude Lévi-Straus being the most famous of this lineage.[25] For film and media studies the most obvious proponent of this type of ethnographic practice is documentary filmmaker Jean Rouch—in particular in his films, *Les maîtres fous* (1955) and *La pyramide humaine* (1961).[26] But for my research I am more interested in the provocative work of anthropologist Marc Augé.

In his short book, *In the Metro*, Augé outlines an ethnographic practice that he suggests could serve as a model for investigating the contemporary culture of Western modernity (and postmodernity) in a variety of settings. Augé, seeking to provide methodological instruction to the novice ethnographer through an examination of the Paris Metro subway system, states:

> The subway corridors ought to provide a good "turf" for the apprentice ethnologist, if only he or she gives up interrogating those who use them (but not chatting with them if the opportunity arises), even worse (horresco referens!), polling them, and is content to observe and listen to them, indeed, to follow them. The apprentice will probably run the risk of gathering clichés (understood here in the strictly photographic sense, as snapshots) and of getting lost in trying to arrange the kaleidoscopic images that at first sight appear arbitrary, disconnected, and baffling. The apprentice can try to classify them by genre; maybe then the resulting inventory will begin to take shape, in a promising way, with a little optimism and imagination; a thousand items recorded, a hundred possible poems, ten future novels—which corresponds to at least three vocations. But stubborn and determined to practice the ethnologist's tasks, the apprentice can then try other classifications, other cross-checks, and begin at the beginning.[27]

Such is the method that I have followed. Now, to begin at the beginning.

1

BLACKBOARD JUNGLE

Narratives of Pedagogy and Experience

> Emotion and memory bring into play a category with which film the-
> ory—and cultural theory more generally—are ill equipped to deal: expe-
> rience. Indeed they have been wary of making any attempt to tackle it,
> and quite rightly so. For experience is not infrequently played as the
> trump card of authenticity, the last word of personal truth, forestalling all
> further discussion, let alone analysis. Nevertheless, experience is undeni-
> ably a key category of everyday knowledge, structuring people's lives in
> important ways.
>
> —Annette Kuhn, *Family Secrets*[1]

Arrival Scenes: Into a Clawing Jungle

At the opening of the film *Blackboard Jungle* (1955), Richard Dadier, the teacher-
protagonist, exits the elevated rail platform, having ridden the train to North
Manual High School in New York City. The landscape he enters is bleak.
Young children play in a funnel of water splashing out of a fire hydrant, evoking myriad photographs depicting urban slum life. Dadier stands seemingly
shell shocked at what he witnesses. As he walks tentatively toward the school,
his figure passes through the frame, momentarily blotting out the signs of decay
and delinquency. He enters the schoolyard through crumbling concrete and
rusted iron gates. Students crowd the yard. Some loiter about, others cavort in
characteristic teenage movie style, dancing and swaggering, they all seem to be
hoodlums. One kid plays with a knife; another kid glares at Dadier as he enters
their territory.

    Another arrival of a different sort: I park my car in the visitor's lot at John
Trauber High School in Vista Valley, California. Although the location is

FIGURE 1.1 Richard Dadier (Glenn Ford) arrives at North Manual High School. *Blackboard Jungle* (Warner Brothers, 1955)

suburban, the city of Vista Valley has a reputation for gangs and a history of animosity between the largely poor Latino community of former migrant farm workers and the largely middle-class Anglo community that runs the city government, police, and school district. A friend who had worked with me in a San Francisco middle school, upon hearing that I had applied for a job at Trauber High, passed along a newspaper clipping that described the stabbing death of a parent at the school. According to the news story, the parent, the father of a student in the school band, had been waiting to pick up his child after an evening concert. As he sat in his car he was confronted by two "gangbanger" boys, and an angry exchange of words followed. During the argument—witnesses said that the disagreement arose from one of the teenage boys sitting on the hood of the father's car—a knife was pulled, and the father was stabbed. He bled to death before an ambulance could arrive. My friend asked me if I really wanted to teach in a district that had such violent students. Of course, this was coming from someone who had spent her entire career as a teacher and administrator in San Francisco Unified, a school district with a troubled reputation of its own.

As I walked across the lot I noticed a group of Latino boys playing basketball in the courts abutting the parking area. They were muscular and tattooed. Sweat dripped from their tanned skin as they roughly jostled each other for position under the basket. Their intense physicality intimidated me, but they for the most part ignored my presence as I passed by. With their shouting and rough play, these young men evoked for me the perpetrators of the father's stabbing no matter how much I told myself that they were totally unrelated to the incident.

Forty years separate the cinematic arrival of Richard Dadier to North Manual High School and my actual arrival at John Trauber. Though fiction, Dadier's arrival is based on author Evan Hunter's experience as a high school teacher in New York City during the 1950s.[2] Both arrival scenes mark a teacher's entrance into a world peopled by otherness. Both arrival scenes activate a set of coded images and discourses concerning the opposition between the adult world of teachers, with conventional notions of morality and reason, and the teenage world of students, with contrary notions of wildness and rebellion (seen from the point of view of adults, but often enough from that of teenagers as well). My knowledge of Trauber and Vista Valley was inscribed with not only the detail of the father's stabbing, but with the ubiquitous images and narratives that portray teenagers (in particular, racialized boys) as menacing and out of control. These boys (these representations of boys) would just as soon knife you as take a look at you.

This otherness, on display as it were, is central to three categories of text that exhibit structural affinities: narrative films that depict teachers and their pedagogical methods, educational ethnographies that incorporate the researcher as subject, and my experience drawn as it were, by the passage of time, into an interpretive space allowing for textual analysis. Although each of these "texts" provides the reader with variable specificities of historical, cultural, and personal "social fact"—each is embedded in that which defines the moment and place—each of these texts also provides for readings that can establish interrelations that form an object of study. Commenting on the narrative tropes that organize historical writing, and which are equally applicable to ethnography, Hayden White states: "In the poetic act which precedes the formal analysis of the field, the historian both creates his object of analysis and predetermines the modality of the conceptual strategies he will use to explain it."[3]

White's suggestion that the object of knowledge must be constructed by the researcher in anticipation of analysis (and importantly his description of this construction as a creative act akin to literature), opens up the possibility that poetic acts (be they in the form of a painting, novel, film, or performance) can be brought to bear on research as objects of knowledge themselves situated within the larger framework of the researcher's predetermined field of inquiry. The macro-object may be the 1950s or juvenile delinquency, but within that constituted area of investigation the film as a micro-object, a totality of events constituted as a narrative, may operate, not as evidence of the event per se, but as evidence of the "mentalities" deployed at that particular moment and as an additional object of inquiry which may help the researcher negotiate the interplay of meanings derived from more traditional sources.[4] For example, that the teens are described as "savages" by several characters within *Blackboard Jungle* does not itself constitute evidence of a social coding of adolescence as menacing Other (or to use the particular theoretical construct from media studies, it does not merely "reflect" the reality of those living in the 1950s). The term *savages* can be read as simply an utterance by a character within a fictional narrative. However, read synchronically against the trailer for *Blackboard Jungle*, the institutional voice of the film, and read diachronically across a selection of teacher-protagonist films from the five decades that follow (which again and again warn of the dangers of uncontrolled or unacculturated youth), the utterances of the fictional characters, one positional expression from a range of "authors" imbricated within a given text, can be read as "in play" with the other forms of discourse on the "savagery" of teens.[5]

In the theatrical trailer for *Blackboard Jungle*, the voiceover breathlessly intones: "Fiction torn from big city savagery," "Teenage terror in the schools," and "It packs a brass knuckle punch in its startling revelation of teenage savages who turn big city schools into a clawing jungle." This voiceover, delivered in a Walter Winchell style, is accompanied by images of robbery, fights, sexual assault, and students dancing in the schoolyard to the strutting rhythm of Bill Haley and the Comets' song "Rock Around the Clock."[6]

This montage of violence and youth subcultural elements is followed by a darkly lit scene in an alleyway in which Artie West (Vic Morrow as the lead teen hoodlum) speaks to Dadier (Glenn Ford as the idealistic teacher): "See, this is my classroom and you're in it. And what I could teach you. First lesson is don't butt in. Don't. Because you'll just flunk out for good." The trailer concludes with a large cover image from the book on which the film was based. This sensational splash image of the book provides the film with authenticity of source: the author knows the truth about teenagers in schools because he spent time as a teacher. The pulpy paperback cover also provides a lurid patina for the authenticity of the source material.

Otherness and Authenticity: Tales from the Field

If otherness, organized as the incongruence between the teenage and adult cultures that operate in educational settings, is one of the tropes that defines representations of teaching, then authenticity of experience is its complement. Arrival scenes both in cinema—again here specifying films that depict teachers as protagonists—and in ethnography seek to foreground these twin attributes. I have already mentioned the approach used in *Blackboard Jungle*—the leering portrayal of the street toughs and the extratextual claims drawing on Evan Hunter's time as a teacher—but these tropes reappear at the opening of many teacher-protagonist films as well as in ethnographies drawn from what sociologist John Van Maanen calls "tales from the field."[7] Van Maanen characterizes ethnographies written in a realist style as erasing the ethnographer from the account of what actually happened during fieldwork. Conversely, confessional ethnographies foreground the experiences of the ethnographer in the field, one of the most infamous being Malinowski's diary written while doing fieldwork in the Trobriand Islands.[8] Impressionist ethnographies "present the doing of fieldwork rather than simply the doer or the done. They reconstruct in dramatic form those periods the author regards as especially notable and hence reportable."[9] As such, cinematic narratives involving teachers often follow patterns set by Van Maanen's category of the confessional ethnography.

For example, the British film *To Sir, with Love* (1968) opens with Mark Thackeray (Sidney Poitier) riding a double-decker bus through swinging London. He arrives at North Quay Secondary School and, in a scene highly reminiscent of *Blackboard Jungle*, happens upon a punk kid, cigarette dangling between his lips, pissing behind a brick wall. Though the title song, sung by the remarkable Lulu, evokes nostalgia for the lost virtues of being a teenager, the film situates Thackeray's students in opposition to him from the outset. While they are hardly savages in the sense projected by *Blackboard Jungle*, Thackeray's students are portrayed as unkempt, unruly lower-class kids bent on resisting school authority and marching toward a stifling life of dead end adulthood.[10] Compared to Thackeray, of the immaculate suit and dignified mannerisms, the students are radically other (interesting in light of the reversal of racial issues—being that most of his students are white and that Sidney Poitier portrayed a street smart tough in *Blackboard Jungle*). The film, based as it is on a novel by West Indian émigré schoolteacher E. R. Braithwaite, grounds its claim to authenticity in an extensive use of location shooting in London and in an explicitly realist style associated with the social problem film, thereby suggesting that what unfolds on screen corresponds closely to the lived experience of schoolteachers and school children in this particular moment and place.[11]

In contrast to the urban setting of *Blackboard Jungle* and *To Sir, with Love*, *Conrack* (1972) takes place in the rural American south. Pat Conroy (Jon Voight) wakes up late, hitches a ride on the back of a junk dealer's truck, and finally arrives at his first teaching assignment as the only passenger on a small boat traveling through the swamp. Although the urban motifs are replaced by those of forlorn grasslands, a one room schoolhouse, and rural poverty—embodied by the young black girl who wordlessly plays hide and seek with Conroy as he disembarks from the boat—the idea of otherness once again defines the relationship between teachers and students. This film positions Conroy's students not as savages (or as rebellious by nature), but as primitives by way of educational underdevelopment. These students are portrayed as gentle, illiterate souls who lack not only education and culture, but also basic necessities such as food and clothing. As in the earlier films, Conroy as the teacher-protagonist must learn to speak through the cultural and social barriers that separate his world from that of his students. But rather than having to transform the tough street swagger that marks the speech of the gang kids from *Blackboard Jungle* and the bubble gum chewing insolence of the East Enders in *To Sir, with Love*, Conroy has to enable a voice for students who are effectively mute. They speak what they can, but they themselves are painfully aware that, in contrast to

Conroy, they are unable to communicate in the language that dominates the world beyond their school. Their academic failure is further confirmed as they are constantly reminded of their "ignorance" by the stern African American female head teacher who refers to them as "babies" although they seem to range in age from eight to sixteen.

In the film *Stand and Deliver* (1987) we meet Jaime Escalante (Edward James Olmos) as he beetles through the LA freeway system in his battered, rusted Volkswagen on his way to the first day of school at Garfield High. Having left his job in the computer industry, he has decided to teach math to inner city high school students. As he enters the parking lot, in an updated version of Richard Dadier's experience, he putts past mobs of students loitering about the front of the school. The mainly Latino students are dominated by boys in oversized pants with colored bandanas wrapped around their foreheads (movie code, if not at the time daily life code, for gang members). The boys talk to one another in harsh slang and glare at Escalante as he makes his way to the principal's office. As Dadier also rapidly discovered, administrators at the school are inept and self-serving. The principal disabuses Escalante of his ideals and sends him immediately to a classroom filled with a group of "sweat hogs" (as they were called in the 1970s' television sitcom *Welcome Back, Kotter*)—students lacking basic literacy and manners, though making up for it in spunk and native wit.

Finally, in two complementary films from the 1990s, *Dangerous Minds* and *187*, the tropes of arrival are altered slightly while continuing to suggest that students are radically other to adults and that the narrative is grounded in the authenticity of experience. *Dangerous Minds* (1995) is based on the experience of former U.S. Marine Louann Johnson (Michelle Pfeiffer) teaching low achieving students in an "academy" program (in this context coded to mean at-risk of dropping out altogether) at Parkmont High School in Palo Alto, California. While Johnson is not shown arriving at the school, her students are depicted leaving their decrepit houses in East Palo Alto to catch yellow school buses, which transport them to the middle-class Parkmont campus across town. In a reversal of the trope of the "civilized" adult entering a world of otherness, the arrival scene in *Dangerous Minds* depicts those who are themselves traditionally Other, arriving en masse to a school whose mainstream students, largely white and middle class, see them, the ethnic Other, as invading *their* territory. This particular trope of otherness displays a dual conceit: Not only are the students Other by virtue of the generational gap, which is further convened by cultural and social difference between themselves and the adults who supervise them, but they are also represented as Other through their racial and economic status in relation to the "regular" clean-cut white kids attending the school.

In the film *187* (1997) the arrival scene is delayed so as to accommodate a narrative preamble in which Trevor Garfield (Samuel L. Jackson) is shown to be a high-strung but dedicated and pedagogically successful science teacher at a run-down, out of control high school in Brooklyn. According to the opening scene, Garfield seems to have developed a student-centered teaching style that connects with most of his "at-risk" students. He brings a bicycle to class and uses it to demonstrate the concept of centrifugal motion. During his class demonstration, Garfield discovers the numbers 187 written in the pages of his course textbook; 187, we are told, is the police code for homicide. Garfield reports the incident to the school principal, who once again demonstrates the incompetence of school administrators (as portrayed in Hollywood narratives) by dismissing the defaced textbook as a prank and attributing Garfield's agitation to his generally nervous demeanor. As Garfield walks down the hall following his discussion with the principal—in a scene shot in highly stylized "slasher" film style—he is brutally stabbed by a student. Garfield crumples to the floor, impaled on a large nail. The student attacker kneels over him and whispers in his ear, as if in a fever dream, the numbers "1, 8, 7."

Thus, the arrival scene in *187* happens fifteen months later, in narrative time, following Garfield's physical rehabilitation as he returns to teaching as a substitute in an East Los Angeles high school. The trope of the arrival scene is now deployed in full. The threatening behavior of the Latino students dominating the schoolyard generates for Garfield a psychological fear drawn from experience as opposed to a generalized anxiety of potential threat as is the case in *Blackboard Jungle*. For Garfield, each of these new students represents the "thug" who actually attacked him at his school in Brooklyn. After many shocking plot twists and much Grand Guignol pleasure,[12] the film concludes with a title that reads, "a teacher wrote this movie." This extratextual utterance is meant, especially in light of the unbelievable violence that pervades the plot, to stamp the film with the weight of authenticity. Regardless of the screenwriter's intentions, the unfortunate message of *187* is that good teachers, despite their best efforts and pedagogical methods, will succumb to savagery— physical intimidation or violence—in response to the uncontrolled force that is the teenage male.

The fact that Garfield reveals himself to be more violent than his students generates an extreme case of "going native," a fear of early anthropologists that after having spent extended time in the field, one would identify too closely with one's informants and thereby lose the objectivity necessary for dispassionate science. The logic of *187* runs as follows: if the students resort to violence, then the teacher must make an example of the students by himself resorting to violence. As in the earlier films, which the tales of Dadier, Thackeray, Escalante, and Johnson highlight, teachers with *good* intentions and *good* pedagogy can, through persistent effort, transform their students into mature, socially adjusted, productive members of the dominant culture. The more recalcitrant students may need to be sacrificed during the process (as in the case of the gang of tough youths that Garfield essentially assassinates), but the consolation is that the majority of students are given the chance to succeed in the world.[13]

Ethnographic Narratives: Parallels and Congruences

Mary Louise Pratt, in her essay comparing ethnography and travel writing, (the "bad object" of rigorous, supposedly scientific ethnography), notes:

> Personal narrative is a conventional component of ethnographies. It turns up almost invariably in introductions or first chapters, where opening narratives commonly recount the writer's arrival at the field site, for instance, the initial reception by the inhabitants, the slow, agonizing process of learning the language and overcoming rejection, the anguish and loss of leaving ... these conventional opening narratives are not trivial. They play the crucial role of anchoring that description in the intense and authority-giving personal experience of fieldwork.[14]

Thus, the arrival scene functions for ethnographic writing much as it does for cinematic teacher narratives.[15] Each of the teacher-protagonist films includes most of the scenes listed by Pratt: arrival at the site, meeting with the site's "inhabitants," learning the language, and overcoming rejection.[16] The teacher-protagonists in these films play out the ethnographic narrative convention of learning the language and overcoming rejection in their attempts to discover the appropriate pedagogical methods for reaching their students. In effect they discover the "right" way to teach their students, much as ethnographers discover the linguistically and culturally correct way of communicating with their research subjects.

In contrast to accounts that focus on educational settings, it is often hard to determine in traditional forms of anthropological ethnography the point at which one has truly entered the field and engaged in observation and interaction with forms of otherness. Anthropologist Paul Rabinow describes his arrival at the field:

> In Morocco only several days and already I was set up in a hotel, an obvious remnant of colonialism, was having my coffee in a garden, and had little to do but start "my" fieldwork. Actually, it was not exactly clear to me what that meant, except that I supposed I would wander around Sefrou a bit. After all, now that I was in the field, everything was fieldwork.[17]

As implied by Rabinow, the field in anthropological work is normally defined as the site of cultural contact with otherness. To enter the field one must abandon the familiar world of daily life by entering into a setting that is "other" by way of its geographical or cultural distance from the familiar home setting of the researcher. This mystique of the field, plunging oneself into the daily existence of an exotic culture (or for the Chicago School, an urban subculture), speaks to the need for an authenticity of experience that forms a correlative between ethnographic practice and popular representations of teaching. The notion of being in the trenches, on the front lines (two dis-tinctly military metaphors), applied to one's time as a teacher complements the idea that one must immerse oneself in the experience of fieldwork. Until one has been in the field (or the trenches of the public school), one is not truly an initiate into the discipline, whether of anthropology or education. One must spend time with the inhabitants of the field and overcome cultural distance in order to be transformed into the anthropologist or the teacher.

Therefore, arrival scenes, similar in structure to those in cinematic teacher narratives, are often inserted at the beginning of educational ethnographies, in particular those written in what Van Maanen designates as the confessional style. For example, Peter McLaren, who had worked as a public school teacher and was working on his doctorate at the time of his research, describes his arrival scene as follows:

> The first thing that struck me when I entered the school was a picture of His Holiness John Paul II that stood about eye level at the end of the hall. This was, indeed, a Catholic school. Although I had made a profession of faith as a Roman Catholic over seven years ago, this was one of the few times that I had been inside a Catholic school.... I felt strange sitting there in a pair of ill-fitting pressed slacks and a shirt and tie. I felt like a sales-man from Radio Shack. The vice-principal confirmed ... that this school was a "problem" school—one of the big "problem" inner city schools.[18]

Throughout his research narrative, McLaren situates himself as sympathetic to the culture of the students, in contrast to that of the teachers, and exhibits a sense of estrangement from many of the adults, teachers, and administrators whom he meets at the school. It is significant that it is the vice-principal, an institutional voice of the school, who identifies St. Ryan as a "problem school." The terms of otherness—juvenile delinquency and pupil disrespect as implied by the word *problem*—are defined by adults at the school and in turn create a reciprocal need for increased control on the part of teachers and administrators.

By virtue of McLaren's feeling of estrangement, two conflicting research dilemmas arise. In the first case, to gain an understanding of the culture of the school, McLaren concentrates on what he perceives as positive within the subculture that has been developed by students. But in turn, he needs to under-stand the cultural voice of those who dominate the school, the faculty. While his distance from both sets of informants provides for a critical stance regarding what research material he collects at the site, this distance also interrupts and blurs the perspective of those he seeks to understand (by situating otherness as a distance both critical and prejudicial).

In this case, as a researcher from outside the community of teachers, McLaren must learn to read the language of the teachers, filtered through his own back-ground as an educator, as well as that of the students whom he is studying. In a scene that could have been lifted directly from *Blackboard Jungle*, McLaren describes a comment by a teacher that he overheard at the school: "[A] teacher had once taught in a school where a pregnant teacher was kicked in the stomach by students ('who were looking for a good laugh') and lost her baby."[19]

While this form of demonization of students by teachers is most likely common, due to structural determinants that constrain the agency of teachers within traditional educational settings, the utterances by particular teachers and administrators serve to demonize the adults themselves within McLaren's narrative. Just as Dadier, Thackeray, Escalante, and Johnson are situated as heroic figures by virtue of their centrality to the plot, ethnographers, perhaps unintentionally, become the heroes of their own narratives as their subject position becomes the teller of the tale.[20] This is not to suggest that McLaren's ethnographic source material is simply biased through his identification with his student informants, but rather that the above excerpt of teacher talk may have causes beyond a simply pusillanimous morality on the part of adults at St. Ryan's.

Similarly, in a short ethnographically informed recollection of his time as a teacher at a middle school in Brooklyn, Peter Sipe relays:

> I remember being repulsed by colleagues who referred to their students as "bitches," "assholes," and "animals," to name but a few epithets. But given the oppositional atmosphere of our school, this same dehumanization strategy is perhaps a natural, if extremely distressing, reaction to the circumstances: If a disruptive student insults you, what does it matter? After all, he or she is just an "asshole." And if your students do not learn, well, it is because they are "animals."[21]

I am not suggesting that the tropes of the teacher-protagonist films directly influence the narratives that arise within the teaching profession (as Pratt suggests that there are direct influences on ethnography by the earlier forms of travel writing), but rather that stories from the teachers' lounge and those from teacher-protagonist films are informed by the same structural conditions that ground the narratives of each. As John Weakland comments in discussing the use of fiction films by anthropologists, "Film patterns and cultural patterns usually are seen largely in terms of parallels and congruences, rather than inferring cause-and-effect relationships."[22] The notion of otherness arises because the social and cultural conditions of otherness are present in the field at the point of "primary sociality" (those social determinants that, when combined with agency, construct the self) that defines both the educational and the ethnographic setting. The structural similarities between the ethnographer and the teacher shape the possible narratives that may be inscribed during such encounters.—higher education as a formal condition of entrance to the field, conventionally white teacher and nonwhite subject population, and a border experience between that which is defined as familiar and that which is defined as not familiar. By extension, those who craft the narratives in which teachers engage with otherness, the filmmakers and producers, are themselves formed by structural determinants generated by the same forces that shape the social conditions of education and ethnography; what Bourdieu calls "dispositions."[23]

In each of the teacher-protagonist films and educational ethnographies discussed so far, the arrival scene positions the narrative voice, whether explicitly present or implied by discourse, as "us"—we are to identify with the travails and successes of the narrator—and the objects of study or teaching as "other." This gulf that divides the teacher-ethnographer from student-informant is what drives the narrative. Each moment of distance offers the opportunity for the teacher-ethnographer to bridge the divide between subject studying and cultural formation studied to eventually conclude the narrative by understanding, by decoding, the shape of a culture identified by its otherness. The arrival scene sets the alpha point of the narrative: we, the audience, comprehend the distance that must be overcome to ensure the goal of understanding. The pedagogical breakthrough, the narrative transition from otherness to communication and understanding, marks the discovery of the correct method to use for teaching one's students.

As a final example within the literature of ethnography, Elenore Smith Bowen in her "fictional" account of her time spent researching a tribe in Africa describes the uncertain, and at times emotionally painful process of breaking through the linguistic and cultural barriers that separate her from her research subjects. Although written in the form of an "anthropological novel," much as the teacher-protagonist films are fictional accounts drawn from the experiences of actual teachers, her narrative reveals insightful parallels to that of Dadier and his fellow teacher-protagonists:

> In the same way that a grunt meaning "yes" in my own language meant "no" in theirs—a very simple reversal which nonetheless got me into one awkwardness after the other—many of the things I did meant one thing to me, something quite the contrary to them. I could only hope that I would do nothing irreparable while I was feeling my way.[24]

By substituting the urban school setting for the dense thicket of African bush, one may draw comparisons between the experience of adult educators, bringing their culture of authoritative adulthood to youth, and the European researcher, bringing her cultural and linguistic baggage to tribal communities. Here is the point at which the craven language of the blackboard "jungle" most closely intersects with that of the well-intentioned, yet culturally blinkered, ethnographer.

Pedagogical Breakthroughs: "What's the Answer, Visual Education?"

For Richard Dadier "the slow, agonizing process of learning the language and overcoming rejection," as Mary Louise Pratt[25] calls the act of overcoming a

FIGURE 1.2 Dadier lectures his students on the fine points of English grammar. *Blackboard Jungle* (Warner Brothers, 1955)

sense of otherness in unfamiliar settings, bears down hard during his first few weeks as a teacher. He begins his time at North Manual High School by relying on the most conventional of teaching approaches, the lecture. In one scene, he scrawls large swaths of the blackboard with fill-in-the-blank examples of well-written English and queries his students regarding the basics of grammar. In response, his recalcitrant students crack smart about his name, referring to him as "Daddy-oh," and refuse to answer his questions correctly.

A new math teacher at the school, Josh Edwards (Richard Kiley), confesses to Dadier during an evening spent drinking at a local bar that he plans to bring his prized collection of 78 rpm jazz recordings to school for use in a lesson. Dadier suggests that the students might not understand the intricacies of jazz instrumentation and Josh blithely asks how anyone could fail to hear the beauty and meaning of jazz. He reminds Dadier that music is all about mathematics and that by "jazzing" up his instruction he hopes to motivate his students to learn more about math.

The following day Josh brings his collection to class. As he stands at the back of his room selecting which records to play, a group of students enter. They taunt Josh and begin to toss his prized 78s in a sadistic game of "keep away." The inevitable result ensues with a large portion of Josh's collection lying dashed and broken on the floor. Josh kneels sobbing amongst the shards of his beloved jazz recordings. For Josh this is a devastating "rejection" by the students (though he does explicitly state that he had brought the records to play for his "more advanced students," in effect insulting the tough street kids from Dadier's class). Thus, the first attempt at using popular culture as an inroad to instruction ends in disaster, and Josh Edwards vanishes from the narrative of

Blackboard Jungle—the distance between him and the students of North Manual High now insurmountable, Edwards having done something "irreparable" in Bowen's sense.

Yet in Josh's misguided attempt at using his enthusiasm for music as a spur to instruction lies the impetus for Richard Dadier's "pedagogical breakthrough." Pushed to the breaking point by the cynicism of his fellow teachers and the incompetence of his principal, Dadier transforms his teaching by using Josh's insight regarding popular media and culture (although in turn realizing that jazz does not speak to his students—their music is rock 'n' roll). In a scene significant from both a narrative and pedagogical perspective, Dadier screens an animated film version of the Jack and the Beanstalk fairy tale for his class. The film is shown in the classic educational film style on a small standalone screen in the front of the classroom with the 16 mm projector operated by Dadier at the back. Students laugh and comment as the film unreels.

Dadier shuts off the projector and opens the blinds while asking students to offer their thoughts on the film. All but one of the students, Vic Morrow's unrepentant street tough Artie West, respond enthusiastically. Dadier suggests that by stealing the magic harp and killing the giant Jack has committed a crime:

Pete Morales (a student): It was only some stinking giant anyway.
Dadier: Why don't you like the giant, Morales?
Student 1: Because he's a giant.
Dadier: You're a Dodger fan, is that right? No kidding fellows. I mean you don't like the giant because he's different than anybody else.
Student 2: That's right.

FIGURE 1.3 Dadier screens an animated film for his students (including Vic Morrow and Sidney Poitier). *Blackboard Jungle* (Warner Brothers, 1955)

Dadier: But is that right? I mean is it right to dislike somebody just because he's different? I mean there are a lot of us right here in this classroom, we're different than anybody else.

Student 3:   If the story is so cockeyed, then what's the point of it?

Dadier: Now we're getting somewhere. Now all your lives you're going to hear stories. What some guy tells you, what you see in books and magazines, on the television and radio, what you read in the newspapers. But, if you can just examine the story…. Look for the real meaning. And most of all fellows if you'll just learn to think for yourselves.

The bell rings, and students continue enthusiastically adding comments to the discussion as they leave the classroom. One student even suggests that he might one day become a movie critic.

As Dadier rewinds the film, two of his fellow teachers, Lou Savoldi (David Alpert) and the cynical Jim Murdock (Louis Calhern), enter the room amazed at Dadier's success with his normally disrespectful and disruptive students.

Savoldi: So, you finally got through to them?

Dadier: I think so. Yes, for once, for the first time.

Savoldi: What's the answer, visual education?

Dadier: Yeah, partly. If you can just get them stimulated.

Murdock: Sure, they'll go for movies, but will that teach them to read?

These two scenes from *Blackboard Jungle*, along with the Josh Edwards preamble on the dangers of failing to consider the cultural specificity of one's

FIGURE 1.4 Dadier discusses the merits of visual education with his colleagues (Louis Calhern and David Alpert). *Blackboard Jungle* (Warner Brothers, 1955)

students, deftly illustrate several key pedagogical positions involving the use of film and media in an educational context. For many film historians the use of film in secondary schools, and educational film in particular, is merely a footnote to the more enlivening history of Hollywood and global narrative cinema (or at best marginalia within the study of documentary or avant-garde film practice). Of course, this submerged film history, that of visual education, opens onto historical pathways that lead directly to the institutionalization of film studies as an academic discipline.[26] While the evaluation of the quality of films used and the implications of these for the most part industrial productions for film history as a whole are not at issue here, in this context it is important to point out that the above scenes directly address the confluence of otherness and experience discussed earlier. Dadier's use of the cartoon film leads to his transformation from the teacher as institutional opponent of his students to his new role as ally and accomplice of these same students.

This idea of a "pedagogical breakthrough" marks a key narrative point in each of the films surveyed during our discussion of the tropes of the arrival scene. Mark Thackeray in *To Sir, with Love* discovers that by engaging his students in discussions of popular culture (in particular music and dance) as well as aspects of their daily lives he can encourage his students to do better in other parts of class instruction. Pat Conroy in *Conrack* discovers that through humor and horseplay his students pay attention to his lessons and participate in assignments. Jaime Escalante in *Stand and Deliver* discovers a method for teaching fractions that features a fry cook costume and a meat cleaver. Louann Johnson discovers that by tossing a tough kid on the floor using her marine-trained judo skills she gains her students' respect (which enables her to teach her lessons, such as they are). Each of these teaching methods, which involve stepping outside of conventional approaches to instruction, foregrounds the interests and experiences of the students in these particular teachers' classrooms. These pedagogical discoveries are depicted not only as solutions to the problems of student motivation, but equally as dramatic turning points in the narrative. Following these turning points, there are still further plot complications, but from this point forward in the narrative the teacher-protagonists in the films surveyed have "connected" with a significant portion of their students, and this allows them to find the key to teaching those students who are initially unruly.

Although each of these scenes can be taken as merely a fictional bit of narrative plot development, each also can be read as indicative of normative approaches to the use of film and popular culture in the classroom. Dadier's use of the cartoon film in *Blackboard Jungle* functions to illustrate a historical pedagogical practice that for the most part has been ignored by film scholars (and for that matter most educational historians).[27] Bowen's novel leads ethnographers to a detailed examination of the practice of fieldwork in its lively retelling of her own time in the African bush, and Richard Dadier's breakthrough pedagogical moment allows for an examination of the methods of "visual"—read film—education during the 1950s. The dialogue between Dadier and his students also speaks to the forms of adult and youth interaction that were available to the imaginations of both filmmakers and teachers during this same period, and in many ways it remains the formula for depictions of the teacher–student relationship to this day.[28]

Critical Media Pedagogy: "Learn to Think for Yourselves"

At first, Dadier's use of the 16 mm cartoon film seems to be explicitly allied with educational proponents who advocate for media being used strictly as a supplemental tool for instruction. This position, broadly drawn, suggests that screening popular media can enhance student motivation and encourage greater involvement with curriculum that may normally be seen as uninteresting or irrelevant by underachieving or nontraditional students.[29] For these advocates, popular culture serves as a means to enliven traditional academic subjects—though here Dadier seems to be simply advocating a melting pot version of diversity—and in effect should be transparent in relation to the disciplinary material being taught. While this is a strictly instrumental approach to using popular culture in the classroom, it is important to point out that Dadier's instruction immediately moves from an instrumental to a critical approach favoring a reading of the media as a purveyor of potentially corrupted or distorted messages. The dialogue that he has with his students following the screening implicitly suggests that by linking the instructional content to the daily lives of the students, and by allowing students to reflect critically on topics of concern to them such as crime and authority, Dadier is able to communicate with his students from an intellectually and emotionally more fecund position. Dadier entreats his students, "If you'll just learn to think for yourselves." By demonstrating the ways in which engaging questions can arise from a cartoon "fairy story," as Artie West has it, Dadier models for his students a method for inquiry about their own world.[30]

Dadier's approach to using media and technology for educational goals is given a name, albeit a 1950s version of today's term, by one of Dadier's fellow teachers as they query him about his success: "What's the answer, visual education?" Proponents of "media education" answer that students need to be taught how to read the media in a manner analogous to the way in which they master literacy in composition and literature courses. These educational theorists, who often use the terms *media education* and *media literacy* interchangeably,[31] generally agree that traditional ideas of literacy, based on reading and writing print media, are being superseded by a form of literacy based on "reading" televisual media (and increasingly "writing" using these same media).[32] One group of writers has extended this premise further to suggest that students must be trained in a range of literacies involving visual, verbal, textual, and spatial orientations and have named this approach, "multiliteracies."[33] The use of videogames has also recently garnered considerable attention as a possible new mode of literacy that can open up education to students who bring different learning modalities to the classroom.[34] But as Murdock asks of Dadier, "Will that teach them to read?"

The more radical proponents of media education, drawing on educational methods and theories from critical pedagogy, respond to this criticism of media use in schools by suggesting not only that media "literacy" is a necessary condition of the current social and cultural moment, but that this type of literacy, given equal status with print culture in the schools, could transform society.[35] For these media educators society's dependence on textual mastery excludes those who may have mastered other ways of comprehending the world, such as musical, visual, spatial, or perhaps tactile modes of understanding (obviously, in all of these examples, including those based on media, the term *literacy* is simply a metaphor for a deeper understanding of codes, symbol structures, in the world). In schools, these excluded students most often become the students who fail to achieve traditional academic goals. Regardless of their emphasis, all the proponents of reading the media as an act of literacy value studying the ways in which media producers construct meanings and the social and cultural determinants that constrain and structure those meanings.

In the representative scenes from *Blackboard Jungle*, Richard Dadier teaches *about* the mediated nature of public communication, "You're going to hear stories, what some guy tells you, what you see in books and magazines, on the television and radio," while teaching a lesson regarding diversity and community *with* a 16 mm film. Granted, for Dadier the structures of mediated communication are not the primary focus of his instruction (for the most part he seems to see media as motivational devices, as evidenced by his conversation with his fellow teachers), but nevertheless using media and technology to teach core academic content implies that some critical reflection on the media should be a component of instruction, though the media as such need not be the primary content.

Through his use of the short cartoon film, Dadier begins to develop a loyal following of students among the group of street toughs that orbit Artie West. As is the climatic necessity in Hollywood feature films, the narrative arc of *Blackboard Jungle* resolves through a violent in-class confrontation between Dadier and West (who incidentally wields a switchblade). The remainder of Dadier's class sides with their teacher, and at the conclusion of the scene they help "Teach" escort Artie to the principal's office for disciplinary action. At least narratively, *Blackboard Jungle* suggests that "visual education" can help to bridge the distance between teachers and their students. Similarly, after a long period of cultural confusion and miscommunication with the tribal people whom she studies, Elenore Bowen finds her social situation transformed: "During this same period my relationship to the community also underwent a noticeable change. I was no longer called 'the white woman' I was 'Kako's

European,' sometimes even 'our European.'"[36] Instead of her possessing the villagers as her research subjects, the villagers claimed her as their "European." The act of helping their teacher with the troublesome, and now disgraced, Artie West signals that the students have accepted Dadier as one of their own while according him the status of respect associated with his role within the culture of the school.

And here is where lived experience diverges from cinematic narrative. If I were to attempt to match the dramatic impact of the pedagogical breakthrough scenes in teacher-protagonist films—*Blackboard Jungle* ends with the spectacle of a knife fight—I would need to fashion a thread of narrative transformation that simply does not exist as a singular event in my own experience. But in the multiplicity of events that constituted the transformative moments of pedagogical interaction with my students, lies a corroboration of the fictionalized narratives of Dadier and the other teacher-protagonists. I can trace across the series of events that led to my own pedagogical breakthrough, grounded as it was in the alpha point of my arrival at the school, a summative evaluation of my experience as the media production teacher at Trauber High. Furthermore, I can draw conclusions about the importance of particular pedagogical details to the quality of the educational experience provided to the students.[37] Of course, as I was in my midthirties and the students were in their teens, there remained a formidable interval between us on a social and cultural level. This was never bridged completely, but there were moments when this gap could be jumped. For instance, in my memory, there replays the day when Johnnie, a "bad" gangbanger kid, dropped by my classroom to show off his cherried out 1967 Chevy Impala. Not much of a drama (no knife fight this), but, nevertheless, a key personal and, if read through my current role as researcher, ethnographic experience.

But what of Dadier—the narrative figure who stands for both the educator and the ethnographer? In the depths of despair, a result of his ongoing sense of failure as a teacher, Dadier seeks advice from his university education professor. As they walk the grounds of a model high school, they observe students busily conducting science experiments and singing the "Star Spangled Banner." Dadier's university mentor turns to him and asks why he doesn't leave North Manual and get a job at a school like the one he is being shown. Dadier responds by returning the viewer to the central metaphor of the film. He says, "I think I'll take another crack at my jungle." As ethnographers pride themselves on their ability to breach the gap between sameness and otherness through narratives grounded in direct experience, teaching narratives organize their stories along similar lines using the tropes of arrival and discovery. The "jungle" is at once a semiotic of wild and uncontained otherness, through the site of the rundown school and the figure of the unconstrained youth, and the generative source of transformations that provide teachers, as they do ethnographers, with a sense of having taken on challenges that justify one's work within the disciplinary institutions of education and anthropology.

As has been suggested throughout this chapter, a comparative analysis of teacher-protagonist films and the ethnographic tropes of otherness and authenticity as applied to education opens up the discourses of media and education to a broader cross-disciplinary understanding along both historical and literary analytical lines. Data drawn from fictional sources do not provide one with "evidence," much as one must continue to suspect data derived from a written exposition of an ethnographer's experience in the field. What an ethnographically oriented approach to film and media education—an anthropologically informed *"explication de texte"*[38]—can do, as demonstrated in an abstracted sense by the scene from Dadier's practice in *Blackboard Jungle*, is to help organize the tropes of experience, rendered as text by time, into a coherent frame of reference from which to understand the ways in which the social and cultural institutions of the media and education seek to authenticate, while often undermining through habitual representation, the roles of teachers and youths in and out of school.

To conclude the discussion of *Blackboard Jungle*, I want to present one final bit of dialogue from the film. As Dadier and his mentor teacher, Professor Kraal, stroll through the model high school, they discuss Dadier's motivation for entering the teaching profession given the bleakness of his current situation at North Manual High.

Professor Kraal: Tell me Richard, why do you want to be a teacher? Just to earn a living? [...]

Dadier: No, hardly. No, I want to teach. Most of us want to do something creative. I can't be a painter, or writer, or an engineer, but I thought that if I could help to shape young minds. Sort of sculpt lives. And by teaching I'd be creating.

The next chapter will explore this notion of the teacher as a creator, the idea that pedagogy is a performance, a form of agency in the world of education, drawing upon a curricular script that is shaped, of course, by the policies of public education, the history of schooling, and the condition of adolescence. The notion of teaching as creative action, as a production, buttresses all of the iterations of pedagogical agency that arise as teachers (and their proxies) and students interact with screens during instruction.

2

AGENTS, SCREENS, AND MACHINES

The Production of Pedagogy

> My concept [of pedagogy] is somewhat wider than the relationships that go on in schools. Pedagogic practices would include the relationships between doctor and patient, the relationships between psychiatrist and the so-called mentally ill, the relationships between architects and planners. In other words, the notion of pedagogic practice which I shall be using will regard pedagogic practices as a fundamental social context through which cultural reproduction-production takes place.
>
> —Basil B. Bernstein, *Pedagogy, Symbolic Control, and Identity*[1]

Teaching Screens: Slate, Celluloid, Raster, Pixel

Snapshot 1967

Diana Harper stands at the front of the classroom facing her students. They sit at their desks in orderly rows. Behind her is a slate blackboard scrawled across with handwriting in white chalk. She walks up and down the rows, gesturing with a piece of broken chalk as she calls on students to answer questions reviewing the day's lesson on the American Progressive era. At intervals, she returns to the blackboard and scratches out more notes for the students to copy into their worn spiral notebooks. Her notes are a mix of key phrases, diagrams, and drawings. Most of her students diligently copy what she has written. A few gaze absentmindedly out the window.

Sometimes while writing on the board, Mrs. Harper's body momentarily blocks the blackboard. Students squeal for her to move, "we can't see what you're writing!" Having heard the complaint many times before, she calmly moves to one side allowing the impatient teens to catch up on their note taking.

At the conclusion of the lesson, she writes the homework assignment at the top right corner of the blackboard, being careful to use her most legible printing. The bell signaling the end of the class session sounds, and as the students leave the room, she quickly erases the board so as to prepare for her next group of students.

Snapshot 1974

Todd Austin watches as his student "film monitor" positions the 16 mm projector at the rear of the classroom and threads the film through the projector's gate. While another student sets up the iridescent movie screen at the front of the class, Mr. Austin, standing to one side, introduces the instructional film that his freshman biology class is about to watch. He cautions that the subject matter is very serious, that it depicts the "miracle of childbirth," and, anticipating the guffaws and wisecracks to follow, reminds his predominantly male class that "I will turn off the movie and we will complete the questions at the end of the chapter, if you prove to be too immature to watch this kind of show."

Mr. Austin takes his position in the back of the class sitting in a folding chair next to the film projector. He scolds a boy, several desks forward, who has already begun to chat with friends. Responding to the glares of his peers, the boy promises to be quiet, so Mr. Austin cues a student to switch off the overhead fluorescent lights as he switches on the projector. During the first ten minutes, students whisper to one another while seeming mostly bored by the film's microscopic images of sperm and fallopian tubes. But as the moment of birth nears, students giggle at the pregnant mother's ballooning stomach and crack jokes about the dated hairstyles in evidence throughout the film.

Frustrated with their childish behavior, Mr. Austin returns to the front of the room and stands so as to block the screen with his body. The film continues to play as he admonishes the students, "if you can't all keep quiet during this movie we won't watch another one for the rest of the year." Students laugh hysterically as the baby's head, born onscreen at that moment, appears to emerge from the front of Mr. Austin's white oxford shirt. Partly amused by his own poor timing, partly exhausted from having to nag his students, Mr. Austin returns to his post at the back of the room and allows the film to finish. Some students take intermittent notes, but for most the experience of watching a movie in class is simply a reprieve from more rigorous coursework such as the lecture and note taking exercise carried out by Mrs. Harper.

Snapshot 1985

Teresa Stanton switches on a television monitor precariously strapped to a rickety, wheeled cart. A loud hiss deafens students as video "snow" appears on screen. Ms. Stanton fumbles with the remote control, lowering the volume as she slides a videocassette into the VCR bolted to the lower shelf of the television cart. A fuzzy VHS image, bleeding reds and greens, fills the screen. She increases the volume as the opening credits from Franco Zeffirelli's film *Romeo and Juliet* scroll past. The students having just struggled through a reading of Shakespeare's play (proving difficult by way of unfamiliar language), Ms. Stanton has decided to reward their efforts by showing them the movie version popular with many teachers of English Literature.

Whereas the short educational film on human reproduction shown in Mr. Austin's class was part of the formally approved curriculum at his school, by using *Romeo and Juliet* (1968) rented from her local video store, Ms. Stanton can no longer rely on a de facto assumption of administrative support for her use of media in the classroom. The film's explicit depiction of teenage sexuality, a 1960s updating of the original, combined with the flash of Romeo's naked buttocks and Juliet's exposed breast necessitate that Ms. Stanton secure permission from parents prior to screening. Without the appropriate "permission slips" on file, Ms. Stanton risks being reprimanded by school administrators and opens the school up to possible lawsuits from disapproving parents.[2] A few of her students have failed to get their parents' permission, or simply lost the slips that were sent home, so Ms. Stanton sends them to the library to do "bookwork," a subtle form of incentive to remember their permission slips for future screenings. Those who remain become quickly enthralled by the movie, while Ms. Stanton sits at her desk grading essays and doing other paperwork. Her desk is positioned at the front of the classroom so as to allow her to watch for unruly students, and to discipline them if the need arises.

Snapshot 1997

John Kressman moves through the computer resource lab observing students as they complete their first HyperCard stack.[3] Each student, as part of the assignment, has interviewed someone from the local community who recently immigrated to the United States. To enliven their projects, Mr. Kressman has required that students photograph their research subjects and collect images that relate to these subjects' life stories. Mr. Kressman looks over the shoulder of a sixteen-year-old girl as she digitally pastes text next to a MacPaint image of the Chinese flag.[4] Mr. Kressman asks where she found the image, and she responds that she copied it from her U.S. history textbook.

Across the room another student erupts with anguished cries as his computer screen freezes once again. Mr. Kressman walks over, reaches around behind the upset student's Apple Mac and hits the restart button. The screen goes black then begins to reboot, a process that takes several minutes to complete. Mr. Kressman asks the young man to be patient and then moves to the whiteboard near the classroom door.[5] He calls for student attention as he begins to explain the procedure for saving student work and for backing up files to a designated server. Simultaneously with his whiteboard presentation, he demonstrates the process on the teacher computer which projects onto a large screen hanging at the front of the classroom. Most students, having lost many hours of work sometime during the process of developing their HyperCard stacks by failing to properly back up, pay close attention to Mr. Kressman's instructions. Of course, some continue to fiddle with their projects while others daydream and stare blankly at the computer monitor in front of them. Mr. Kressman glares at one student who fails to look up from his monitor and even fails to notice the admonishing glance. Other students, who are paying attention and are annoyed at the interruption, call out in unison to the oblivious student, "Robert, Mr. Kressman is talking!" Embarrassed, Robert finally looks up, and Mr. Kressman finishes his explanation on how to save files.

The Remediation of the Blackboard

Although these vignettes are composite narratives based on memory, experience, and observation, each represents a model of instruction dependent on a teacher interacting with a screen.[6] And while each narrative is specific to a historical moment, each could just as easily stand for instructional practices evident slightly earlier or later than the date indicated (save for the blackboard which has had a long and storied history in education). Furthermore, each of the screens depicted manifests specific visual attributes that typify particular modes of instruction constructed through the specificity of the interaction between teacher and screen.

Prior to the 1990s, the blackboard was the dominant visual element in the typical classroom in an American school (other than the body of the teacher, which fails to register its visuality as a result of the seeming naturalness of the fully present body). But, for the most part the blackboard has generated little discussion by educational theorists as they situate the screen technologies that have been seen as enhancing (and at times, undermining) pedagogy over the past fifty years. Visual aids in the form of posters, filmstrips, 16 mm films, videos, and computers have all had their proponents and detractors, but the ubiquitous blackboard, that most obvious of screens, has generated little in the way of analysis. Media theorist Marshall McLuhan, while discussing his famous dictum "the medium is the message," refers to the electric light as a communication medium that in many ways mirrors the blackboard as a pedagogical medium:

> The electric light escapes attention as a communication medium just because it has no "content." And this makes it an invaluable instance of how people fail to study media at all. For it is not till the electric light is used to spell out some brand name that it is noticed as a medium. Then it is not the light but the "content" (or what is really another medium) that is noticed.[7]

Blackboards are the primary screens of education; the technology of teaching most simply elegant in function. The blackboard allows for instantaneous inscription (McLuhan's content), a visual-textual counterpoint to the living presence of the teacher. As questions are answered and statements are made, a corresponding trace is made on the surface of the blackboard. Explicitly this running commentary cues note taking, but implicitly the marks also signal to students the thought processes of the teacher. These thoughts may be prefigured in the lesson notes (whether in an exhaustive way or as merely indicators of the structure of the argument), nevertheless, in a particularly dynamic lecture these notations serve as a guide through instruction and as spurs to further thinking on the part of the student. But regardless of its use by individual teachers, the blackboard by virtue of its ubiquity and commonsense functionality in everyday instruction seems to preclude thoughtful consideration of its remediation by all of the instructional screens that have followed and that pervade educational settings throughout the late twentieth and early twenty-first centuries.

New media theorists Jay David Bolter and Richard Grusin, while extrapolating from McLuhan's notion that "the 'content' of any medium is always another medium,"[8] suggest that this reliance of newer media upon previous media for content should be described as "remediation"—and here, consistent with McLuhan's formulation, we are considering the social uses of media. "We call the representation of one medium in another remediation, and we will argue that remediation is a defining characteristic of the new digital media."[9] As we shall see, the "new digital media" figure prominently in the latest version of educational media and technology, but the case can be made that earlier media, in particular films and television, either modeled their pedagogical approach on the uses of the blackboard or represented the blackboard as a teaching technology within the "content" of their educational programming. Consequently, all the screens that follow on the blackboard—those of overhead projector, film, television, video, and computers—should be seen as explicitly remediating the pedagogical and aesthetic functions of the blackboard in the reified space of media.

But the remediation of the blackboard, like the forms of remediation described by Bolter and Grusin, develops from the logistical mandates of teaching as much as it does from the mediation of the screen itself. Teachers have come to rely on the blackboard because it has proven to be the most convenient and efficient source of visual and textual information during instruction (even as new technologies have promised increased convenience while demanding more preparation time from the teacher). Educational historian Larry Cuban suggests that common pedagogical uses of the blackboard reflect the functional conditions that have determined conventional approaches to instruction in most American schools:

Lecturing, recitation, seatwork, and homework drawn from texts are direct, uncomplicated ways of transmitting knowledge and directions to groups. Given the constraints placed upon the teacher by the daily schedule and the requirements that a course of study be completed by June, these instructional practices permit the teacher to determine, in a timely and efficient manner, whether or not students have learned the material.[10]

Cuban goes on to say that, considering the mandate placed on teachers to instruct large groups of students in short segments of time, the blackboard (and the textbook) "have been simple, durable, flexible, and responsive to teacher-defined problems in meeting the demands of daily instruction."[11] Unlike the blackboard (always available as an aid to instruction), filmstrips, 16 mm films, and television became special occasions for instruction and not the daily norm. The filmstrip projector, with its familiar "beep" signaling the teacher to advance the frame (still a nostalgic sound for a certain generation), had to be taken out of the supply closet, set up in the back of the classroom for use, and then returned to its case for storage. The 16 mm film projector and the television set had to be scheduled with an audiovisual technician in advance and then had to be delivered to the classroom at the appropriate time by either the technician, or as in Mr. Austin's case, by a specially trained student film monitor (a position that might be rewarded with either respect or a bloody nose).

In the case of television, instruction needed to be "programmed" around the appropriate broadcast, so that the structure of class time was disrupted both by the arrival of the hardware and the timing of the program to be screened. Thus the blackboard is the teaching screen most accommodating to preexisting methods of instruction as described by Cuban.[12] And while Cuban explains the failure of later screen technologies through a lack of coherence with the demands of the school setting, he only briefly mentions the ways in which teachers, and educational designers, have remediated the blackboard through electronic and digital technologies (absent, of course, Bolter and Grusin's specific terminology).[13]

While the value of the blackboard relies on its flexibility and simplicity of use during instruction, it remains important to look at what it lacks so as to understand the ways later educational media remediate the blackboard. While teacher-drawn sketches on the blackboard or photographs tacked to the wall can provide students with varying degrees of visualization concerning the people, places, objects, and such described in lectures and class discussions, films and television can extend student visual comprehension of subject material with time-based images. Films, by virtue of scalable projection, can supplement the visual space of the classroom with an image comparable in size to that of the blackboard (obviously with the benefits of sound as well), while television can lend a sense of liveness to historical and contemporary events on a screen that was, until recently, limited in visibility due to the small size of most video monitors.[14]

Many early educational television programs—notably *Sunrise Semester* (1957–1982) on the Columbia Broadcasting System (CBS) and *Continental Classroom* (1958–1963) on the National Broadcasting Company (NBC)—featured course content structured around formal lectures supplemented by an onscreen blackboard. For many students, to experience these broadcast lectures was to watch a box containing a miniaturized version of the classroom in which they were sitting. But more importantly, the pedagogical encounter modeled on these programs derived as much from traditional documentary film practice as from classroom teaching. *Sunrise Semester* and *Continental Classroom* put a face to the documentary voiceover that had been featured in the majority of educational films and television programs and that face belonged to the university lecturer accompanied by illustrative visuals and text incorporated into the tiny budgets for both shows by making extensive use of the blackboard.[15] As Mrs. Harper guided students through key concepts by scrawling them across a blackboard, professor-hosts on *Sunrise Semester* used the blackboard in the studio to similar effect.

By the 1980s, teachers like Ms. Stanton were not limited to showing short films produced specifically for the educational market or Hollywood films condensed to fit the time structures of the school day as Mr. Tamberlin had been during the mid-1970s. The rented videocassette began to replace teachers' reliance on the 16 mm films that had dominated media in the schools for the previous twenty years (with the exception of isolated instances of school districts that experimented with educational television programming [ETV]).[16] Consequently, feature films screened on videotape increasingly became rewards for work accomplished and positive in-class behavior in addition to the strictly instructional uses to which media had been previously put. Often schools made use of a single video monitor and deck combination strapped to a wheeled cart modeled on the way in which film projectors had been circulated throughout schools. However, due to large catalogs of instructional films archived at city and county educational media services departments, a symptom of the bureaucratic structure of public schooling, 16 mm films lasted as a primary source of media-based instruction well into the 1980s.

At John Trauber High School in 2003, the supply clerk, who also served as the school's 16 mm projector checkout person, explained that the district had finally decided to stop repairing the school's single remaining film projector due to the fact that no one had requested its use for the past three years. And as part of a district-wide technology bond levy in the mid-1990s (which passed overwhelmingly), Trauber High installed television monitors and video cassette recorders in every classroom as well as a video retrieval system run by the school's media specialists, formerly librarians, which allowed teachers to show cable and video programming using a classroom remote. This system provided the immediacy of the blackboard for supplemental visual instruction (instantaneous playback and broad choice of programming), but was never adopted widely by teachers as a result of its poorly designed and difficult-to-learn user interface.

By the early 1990s, computer labs were available for teachers to use during instructional time and often for after-school tutoring and class preparation. Video remained the main form of media in the classroom, although it still, for the most part, operated as supplemental to the main forms of instruction centering on lecture, project-work, textbooks, class discussions, and the blackboard (or whiteboard). And for the most part, computer labs constrained instruction in ways equally disruptive to classroom time as those encountered while using television and 16 mm films. Teachers still had to compete with one another for access to technology whose use necessitated breaks in class instruction while taking time to either set up equipment or move students to another location.

With the introduction of digital technologies, the remediation of the screen bifurcated. The teacher's computer screen projected large during instruction operates in ways similar to the blackboard (as when Mr. Kressman demonstrated for students how to save their work to the server), but the student computer screens, at work carrels or on a specified number of machines in the back of a classroom, operate more on the model of the notebook used by students during conventional moments of note taking.[17] The teacher continues to dominate the space of instruction during large screen projection in ways similar to that of the blackboard-dependent classroom by virtue of the teacher-delivered lecture and lesson plan. But what has changed is that by using standalone or networked computer workstations, the student is given a screen workspace that is independent of the teacher (there are computer applications that control workstations, but students most often resent and resist this big brother style approach).

The large scale projection of the teacher's computer remediates the earlier screen of the blackboard—flexible and responsive, but less durable due to the short life span of most projector bulbs—while also remediating film and television screens through particular iterations of web browser or presentation software. The Internet has increasingly moved, since its inception, toward more cinematic modes of presentation as digital design drifts from a print-based model to one more dependent on motion graphics and filmmaking. Student screens, in ways converging on mobile media and ubiquitous computing, are complementary to the larger screen of the teacher workstation that in the best of situations mirrors the work that is being accomplished by the teacher while retaining some modicum of autonomy for students.

Pedagogical Agents: The Beloved and the Machine

As the blackboard, through the functional ghosting of remediation, haunts the screens of education, the "beloved teacher," evoked by Mr. Tamberlin and Mr.

Dadier, haunts the pedagogical figures that populate the narratives of media and education. But the value of the beloved teacher, admittedly summoned as much from popular culture as from youthful memories, is that it recalls for many people what is most emotionally tangible about education. The underlying intellectual warmth and authoritative guidance associated with a beloved teacher's pedagogy represents, for those who consider it at all, educational discourse at its most powerfully erotic.

The bond that many feel for a fondly remembered teacher in notable ways parallels the complicated interactions that characterize *transference* as it is used in the lexicon of psychoanalysis. Psychoanalysts Laplanche and Pontalis state that:

> When Freud speaks of the transference repetition of past experiences, of attitudes towards parents, etc., this repetition should not be understood in the literal sense that restricts such actualisation to really lived relationships. For one thing, what is transferred, essentially, is psychical reality—that is to say, at the deepest level, unconscious wishes and the phantasies associated with them. And further, manifestations of transference are not verbatim repetitions but rather symbolic equivalents of what is being transferred.[18]

While transference for psychoanalysis is a technical term demarcating a particular transformational moment in the therapeutic setting (the pivotal point at which patients develop an emotional dependence on their therapist and thus "transfer" repressed feelings regarding their father or mother onto the therapist), here I wish to use the term to typify the powerful passions—anger, resentment, love, sexual attraction—that constitute a communicative moment in which the deeply emotional relationship with a beloved teacher originates. Social theorist Anthony Elliot extends the clinical model of transference to broaden the context to include everyday forms of interaction:

> In our emotional attachments to others, from intimate sexual relationships to the organizational structures of authority in public life, the phenomenon of transference is a fundamental dimension of human experience: we people our world ... with emotions and fantasies drawn from the past, but projected onto current experiences.[19]

That the beloved teacher depicted in many cultural representations is often male (seeking to stabilize authority, often in ingenious ways) suggests that the symbolic sign of the father, as deployed most famously by Jacques Lacan, comes into play.[20] The beloved teacher becomes a substitute figure for the absent father, actual or imagined, thereby allowing the infantile desire on the part of the student to seek emotional coherence through the certitude of discipline (after the realization of loss following the separation from the comforting wholeness of the mother). This pattern, no less complicated for being social as well as psychic, overlays the figure of the psychoanalytic therapist with that of the beloved teacher. The relational-communicative bond that works out in the therapeutic setting therefore correlates to the mechanism at work in one's memories of a beloved teacher. Mr. Tamberlin ably inhabits the figure of transference through his affective and cognitive abilities—the cool hipness, the art practice experience, and the visual fullness of his image—all of which evoke his role as the father authority that fails to bite (though in the case of Mr. Dadier, the phallic knife fight between pupil and teacher that concludes *Blackboard Jungle* takes on increased significance in relation to the reconstitution of symbolic authority).

In contrast to the fundamentally psychoanalytic figure of the beloved teacher, there is another figure that has instead been endowed with a technocratic impulse, characterized by some historians as the "technological sublime" of midcentury American culture, the "teaching machine."[21] This figure dredges up for public discourse images of soulless automatons replacing the flesh-and-blood bodies of fondly remembered teachers.[22] Here, programmed instruction (educational jargon for the pedagogical functioning of teaching machines) symbolizes, for a wary public comprised of former students, teaching as a streamlined Fordist process of mass production, absent any affective (or for that matter, cognitive) engagement with students. It is important to note that behavioral psychologist B. F. Skinner, an influential proponent of the use of teaching machines in public schooling addressed the fears of automation directly in his book on teaching and technology:

> The machine itself, of course, does not teach. It simply brings the student into contact with the person who composed the material it presents. It is a laborsaving device because it can bring one programmer into contact with an indefinite number of students. This may suggest mass production, but the effect upon each student is surprisingly like that of a private tutor.[23]

But for the popular imagination, the idea of a teaching machine summons up the numerous dystopias of posthumanism found in science fiction scenarios. The twentieth century fear of automation is perhaps best exemplified in popular culture by the iconic figure of the female robot-Maria in Fritz Lang's 1927 film *Metropolis*.[24] But to understand the suspicion with which the public initially approached the use of technology for instruction, it is important to get a sense of what teaching machines were like for a generation of students who entered public education during the 1950s and 1960s. Skinner's description of a typical teaching machine allows a glimpse at the material form given to programmed instruction in the late 1950s:

> The device is a box about the size of a small record player. On the top surface is a window through which a question or problem printed on a paper tape may be seen. The child answers the question by moving one or more sliders upon which the digits 0 through 9 are printed. The answer appears

in square holes punched in the paper upon which the question is printed. When the answer has been set, the child turns a knob.... If the answer is right, the knob turns freely and can be made to ring a bell or provide some other conditioned reinforcement. If the answer is wrong, the knob will not turn. A counter may be added to tally wrong answers.... When the answer is right, a further turn of the knob engages a clutch which moves the next problem into place in the window.[25]

Skinner's description, cool and formal as it is (and a bit droll in its methodical explication), reinforces humanistic-literary concerns over the dangers of replacing humans with robots as depicted in cinematic science fiction moving from Lang's Maria through Stanley Kubrick's HAL 9000 in *2001: A Space Odyssey* (1968) to the deadpan mannerisms of Agent Smith in the Wachowskis' *The Matrix* (1999).[26] And it signals a moment in which technological devices fail to reproduce human empathy, which is a key component to understanding the emotional affect associated with narratives (and memories) that feature beloved teachers.

Thus, these two figures, the beloved teacher and the teaching machine, set binary points on a spectrum across which span a range of educational agencies. But through this structural binary, thesis and anti-thesis, another figure can be suggested that dialectically integrates the teacher with programmed instruction to form a third figural form which resists negating the specificity of either the beloved or the machine. This new third figure, purloined from research programs in computer science and artificial intelligence (AI), is that of the "pedagogical agent."

The pedagogical agent within AI research, as a virtual human embedded in a digitally constructed environment, incorporates the emotional affect and creative action of the flesh-and-blood teacher with the training orientation and efficiency of programmed instruction. Indeed, this AI inspired notion of agency should broaden our conception of pedagogy to include any intentional act of instruction delivered through or across the many different screens and machines associated with educational media and aligns with the definition of pedagogic practice suggested by sociologist Basil Bernstein, "The notion of pedagogic practice which I shall be using will regard pedagogic practices as a fundamental social context through which cultural reproduction-production takes place."[27]

Pedagogical agents, and their associated pedagogic practices in line with Bernstein's approach, are therefore understood as configured systems composed of a combination of mediated and human actors: technologies plus flesh embedded within a social context. Pedagogical agency exists as a metaphor for expanded notions of what constitutes instruction, but it does so by using an understanding of metaphor as an embodied experiential-conceptual tool that structures action in the sense used by linguists George Lakoff and Mark

Johnson in their work which has been influential on developments associated with particular strands of AI research.[28] In this regard, the pedagogical agent reassembles many of the attributes of the flesh-and-blood teacher within a cultural–educational technosocial space imbricated within entertainment discourse as the dominant form of public pedagogy and communication.

Educational theorists often characterize pedagogy as a realm of discourse distinct from, and often at odds with, the interactions upon which media and entertainment culture depends. For many in education there is a privileging of the act of lecturing or discussion as qualitatively more substantial and serious than what transpires during television news, reality television, and, most certainly, talk radio. But these ephemeral media forms, organized as they are around segmentations of commercial time and the discourses of entertainment, bear down heavily on the performance of instruction. Obviously, the ideas and information professed by the classroom teacher are not those delivered by the network evening news anchor, but both function within the framework for understanding communication suggested by John Dewey:

> Not only is social life identical with communication, but all communication (and hence all genuine social life) is educative. To be a recipient of a communication is to have an enlarged and changed experience. One shares in what another has thought and felt and in so far, meagerly or amply, has his own attitude modified. Nor is the one who communicates left unaffected.[29]

The social life of which Dewey speaks links the lecture hall to the news lead, both of which are negotiated through forms of agency ripe with pedagogical intent (thereby recalling Lord Reith's archly elitist founding mandate for the British Broadcasting Company, "to educate, to inform, to entertain"). And while the mode of the lecture allows for a more interactive moment of communication, the increasingly networked world of contemporary life has begun to smudge the line between the face-to-face interplay of the school and the more one-sided discourse of broadcasting.

By confronting this altered terrain of discourse (from one dominated by a reliance on the lecture to one relying increasingly on cinematic and televisual genres), the pedagogical agent, at once a machine and a representation of an exemplary teacher, opens up the possibility for the creation of future "teaching machines" that bear the affective qualities most of us would mark as deeply human: programmed for instruction, yet emotionally and cognitively complex. This form of virtual human, designed and programmed to provide simultaneously efficient and humanistic teaching, serves as the conceptual figure through which to understand practices that are present equally, although in differing proportions, in the "flesh-and-blood" teacher, the educational television series, and the distance learning software module. Thus, the many determinants that go into delivering instruction resulting from the personality and training of the teacher, the strengths and weaknesses of instructional technology, the policies and mandates of the school administration, or the composition and experience of the student population—in short, pedagogy in its entirety—become constitutive of the pedagogical agent given shape and size as a representational figure. The corporeal form of the teacher (and professor), at once an actually existing person, libidinal fantasy, and "straw man" of public discourse on education, stands in as the physical manifestation of pedagogical agency.

Authors and Agents

Aside from its meaning lifted from research in AI, pedagogical agency also builds upon historically relevant critical work addressing authorship as a form of distributed cognition (or agency) in film and media—in particular auteur-structuralism.[30] One of the earliest approaches in film studies exhibiting methodological rigor, auteur-structuralism sought out work by Michel Foucault and Roland Barthes (amongst others) as entry points for reimagining authorship as a form of distributed agency across discourses or texts (a concept which has received considerable attention in cognitive science research).[31] In his work, Foucault displaced the idea of the "author," a particular imprint of genius upon a text invoking a name and a lineage, with that of the "author function," the totality of possibilities and situations that contribute to the creation of a work of art.[32] By supplanting the individual artist, Foucault expanded the range of discourses available for analysis while contesting previously absolute notions of what made a text worthy of scholarly study.[33]

Film theorist and filmmaker Peter Wollen took up Foucault's notion and applied it to the reciprocal relationship that exists between cinematic authors and filmic texts, and thereby providing a humanistic reading of the sociological insight into the complex interrelationship between practical action and institutional structure.[34] Wollen's contribution to auteur-structuralism as a trend in screen theory attempted to counter the reductive romanticism of film critics, reflected in the evaluative hierarchies of Andrew Sarris that used the popular critical work of the French writers for *Cahiers du cinéma* to build a foundation for understanding American cinema as a form of literature.[35] Contrary to "la politique des auteurs" with its elevation of the director to a position of singular authorship, auteur-structuralists conceived of the "author" named John Ford, the flesh-and-blood individual who directed many successful Hollywood films, as a referent for a form of distributed authorship resulting from a structured aggregation of actions and interactions on the part of cast and crew, which is itself determined, in many instances, by the specificity of Hollywood production methods and power relations. All of these actions and interactions contribute to form an author-figure, a composite derived from the weighted contributions of many creative and institutional agents, which stands in for the actual man named John Ford and accounts for the multiple authorship of Hollywood cinema.

This author-figure, "John Ford," exhibits stylistic tendencies that can be considered as generative of particular films and even of specific genres within the Hollywood system. Each cinematic author in this form of distributed agency—producer, director, actor, set designer, animal wrangler—contributes to the overall contours and shape of the cultural product (network television, independent film, Hollywood movie), but each provides a differential creative input into the overall act of production. The pedagogical agent, as the author-figure within the differently structured field of education, exhibits agency in ways analogous to that ascribed to "John Ford" by auteur-structuralism. The action of an individual teacher or professor may be more akin to the agency exerted by a supporting actor or a lighting technician in the cinematic arena than to that of "John Ford," but the weight of structural determinants on the actions ascribed to creative agents in auteur-structuralism holds. In fact this expanded conception of agency allows for the authorship of fictional agents to be accounted for in the roles upon which they are called to action in the narratives that they inhabit: Richard Dadier as pedagogical agent is at once an extension of actor Glenn Ford, but also a unique participant within the narrative as a schematic representation of the actions available to teachers in urban schools during the mid-1950s.

A fuller conception of the pedagogical agent as a form of distributed authorship can be developed by calling upon Bourdieu's notion of the "field of cultural production." For Bourdieu the field addresses the problematic relationship that exists between agency and the structural determinants on agency while accounting for the unequal and contrary cultural forms that characterize cultural production (as writing, painting, or film directing). Bourdieu refers to studio moviemaking as "the field of large-scale production."[36] In this form of production, agents act with an eye to larger rewards of money and status while being constrained by the preexisting givens of the field of large-scale production subsumed within, and therefore explicitly dependent upon, the larger fields of economic and power relations. Regardless of the specifics of these constraints, within Bourdieu's theorization of the field the authorial figure of "John Ford" results from the confluence of the economic, cultural, inter- and intrapersonal, and professional relations inherent in the interlocking and embedded fields of production and can be said to provide the coherent contours of expression and style within a group of films "signed" by the filmmaker John Ford.

Thus if the author-figure represents a matrix of agency, the pedagogical agent represents the locus point for a confluence of the social, cultural, and economic determinations that ground education as an institution. These determinations construct a "field of educational production," which reflects both Bourdieu's theoretical formation and the current mandate to reorganize higher education along lines giving greater emphasis to technical and professional coursework.

Within this field of educational production, the agency afforded teachers at times resembles the positions encountered within the field of large-scale production (celebrity teachers appearing on *Oprah* and being given MacArthur grants for their genius) while at other times most teachers seem to populate a range of positions in the field, described by Bourdieu, as that of "restricted production." The field of restricted production results when a set of cultural practices fails to generate money, fame, or power in sufficient quantities to qualify as goals in themselves. In place of these quantitative goals, restricted production rewards players with seemingly more freedom of action, more variety of moves within the givens of the game, and increased status with a small but loyal following (as in fan cultures or high art social groupings). Though, for restricted production, too much status and not enough cash can lead to a sense of failure on the part of agents as time wears on with little concrete rewards accruing. "Teacher burnout," an affliction of older teachers who have grown weary over too many years spent with too many recalcitrant students with too little rewards for their efforts, can be seen as the analogous result within the field of restricted production that defines much of publicly funded American education.

But the concept of pedagogical agency should not be seen as diminishing or denying the potency of "feelings" of agency that a given actor in an educational setting may experience. Feelings of individual agency are at once significant and illusory. As with cinematic narratives, certain aspects of agency are inevitable while others remain uncertain. For Bourdieu, social relations interlock, overlap, and influence one another and thereby create a smaller, yet undiminished set of options open to a given player within a given field. And while individual teachers and professors may argue that they are the direct "authors" of their actions, the intentionality of a given teacher marks them as a site for a confluence of possible moves determined by the educational field. Pedagogical agents embody organized discourses constructed through a rough mix of personal and educational histories, administrative hierarchies, written and technological texts, student expectations, and disciplinary norms. The fictional teacher in a film or novel is the creation of the author of a text, and this author is in turn authored by his or her own actions in interaction with the external determinants mentioned earlier. Similarly, the classroom teacher is both author of instruction within the confines of his or her classroom, albeit on a quite limited basis, and is in turn structured by educational bureaucracies in the choice and implementation of his or her curriculum and pedagogy.[37]

If, as Foucault suggests, authorship can include discourse that is not authored in the conventional sense, then the curriculum, lesson plans, and instructional style of individual teachers can be considered as forms of authoring in the world. And this authoring, delimited by the field of educational production and Bourdieu's complementary notion of the habitus[38]—the sense of the game, gathered through birth status and social class that each player brings to the field—constitutes pedagogical agency.

So we move from the moment in which authorship, to use the media studies expression, seems like a determined event, the John Ford moment, to one in which each of the agents are at play in a field in which action develops as structures gain and wane. While not conscious in the sense that is attributable to human agents, machine and screen agents interact with the world in ways that break the limitations on conventional notions of interaction and dialogic discourse. From Foucault's opening up of discourse we have moved to each intentional act representing a petite form of authorship in the world with consequences large and small ensuing—a cultural production of pedagogy.

Modes of Pedagogical Agency

Three modes of instruction characterize pedagogical agency: the teacher presented, the teacher augmented, and the teacher embodied. Each of these modes defines the kinds of interaction that occur between teachers and students as mediated through the technological interface of the screen. The narrative vignettes that began this chapter sketched rough contours for some of the forms of interaction that have been historically available to pedagogical agents in the most common instructional settings (at least within the norms of American public education). Ms. Harper, Mr. Austin, and the others are all authors of their instruction, but in each case the screen—blackboard, monitor, and such—delimits the range of possible interactions between teacher and pupil. In addition, the quality of the interaction between teacher, student, and screen further clarifies the specificity of this relationship, which is at once deeply historical and participatory, and can be visualized spatially as a triad. The teacher (actual or virtual), the student (present or implied), and the screen (blackboard, film, video, or computer monitor) comprise the three sides of a figure indicating this set of relations. What changes in each of the modes of pedagogical agency—presented, augmented, or embodied by a screen—is the greater or lesser presence of technological mediation and the field of educational production that grounds the interplay between each of the constituents.

The Teacher Presented: The Teacher on the Screen

The first mode of pedagogical agency, the teacher presented, subdivides into three variants of the teacher on the screen. The first represents a figure that merely inhabits a narrative as a professional type, such as when a character is employed as a teacher (or, in other instances, as a doctor or a lawyer). The professional career of the character remains incidental to his or her more important role within the narrative as a father, mother, friend, or more significantly for some narratives, secret agent or superhero. For example, in the film *The Substitute*

(1996), Tom Berenger's "Shale" character poses as a substitute teacher named Mr. Smith to enact revenge upon the student thugs who attacked his wife, herself a teacher at the school. Berenger's character's role as a former Special Forces military officer—and angel of vengeance—trumps his role as a teacher. Any pedagogy that is represented on screen, enacted by a character within the conventions of the plot, is merely a form of "stage business" for the characters to enact until the main event occurs, in this case the bloody battle between Berenger and the gang members.

Similarly, in school movies that focus on students as the protagonists such as *Dazed and Confused* (1993) or *Fast Times at Ridgemont High* (1982) the character of the teacher simply serves as part of the humanity peopling the world of the main characters, the students, or as a foil for their pranks and high jinks. In the case of films such as *Our Miss Brooks* (1956), based on a popular 1950s television comedy series, or *Looking for Mr. Goodbar* (1977) the teacher character exists as one of many possible professions that could have been chosen for the narrative, but mostly the choice of setting serves to evoke a nostalgia for the simplicity of school days past and for enactments surrounding the clichés associated with romantic comedy or melodrama. Regardless of the genre in which the teacher character appears, the main emphasis on the development of the character is external to his or her role as a teacher; therefore pedagogy is not present as such.

The second variant of the teacher presented foregrounds the actual pedagogical approach of the teacher depicted onscreen. Dadier's teaching method is not incidental to the plot; instead it represents the dramatic turning point within the film's narrative. Each of the cinematic teacher-protagonists' choice of pedagogical method, as surveyed in chapter 1, defines his or her presence on the screen; that is, Mark Thackeray, Pat Conroy, Jaime Escalante, and Louann Johnson. It is not the intention of the narrative to teach the audience something, yet the methods employed on screen represent the historically situated methods of teaching popular at the time of filming.[39]

The teacher presented in its third variant positions the teacher figure on screen within a narrative with an eye to providing instruction to an imagined audience of students. The initial course offering on the aforementioned *Continental Classroom*, "Atomic Age Physics" featuring University of California, Berkeley physics professor Harvey White, serves as an early example of this approach to the onscreen instructor.[40] Similarly celebrity hosts such as Carl Sagan, *Cosmos* (PBS, 1980), and Jacob Bronowski, *The Ascent of Man* (BBC, 1973), provide onscreen pedagogy in the form of miniature lectures with traditional "voice of god" documentary voiceovers filling in the details of the topic at hand. This third variant of the teacher presented will be examined in more detail in chapter 3 by focusing on *French in Action*, a French language and culture telecourse developed by Yale Professor Pierre Capretz for public television affiliate WGBH in Boston during the 1980s.

The Teacher Augmented: The Teacher and the Screen

The second mode of pedagogical agency, the teacher augmented, characterizes the pedagogy delivered by a flesh-and-blood teacher in conjunction with a form of screen media—commonly an educational documentary, an audiovisual illustration, or a digital slideshow presentation. Whereas the relation between teacher, student, and media in the teacher-presented mode embeds the visual representation of the pedagogical agent within the media apparatus to create a virtual triangulation of interaction, the teacher-augmented mode concretizes this relationship as a three sided interaction—flesh-and-blood teacher, student, and media screen—in the actual life-world of instruction (the instructional *Lebenswelt* according to the terminological frame of phenomenology).

This configuration of human coupled with technology may most readily evoke for those in media and cultural studies Donna Haraway's influential notion of the cyborg.[41] However, a more apt, and disciplinarily precise, reference comes by way of educational theorist Howard Gardner and his work on the ways that traditional approaches to educational research fail to account for the distributed nature of learning. Drawing upon research in cognitive science, he suggests that: "Nearly all learning…take[s] place in one or another cultural context; aids to [a student's] thinking will reside in many other human beings as well as in a multitude of cultural artifacts. Far from being restricted to the individual's skull, cognition and intelligence become distributed across the landscape."[42]

Richard Dadier's use of the cartoon films, while fictive, suggests a move from a pedagogical form dominated by the knowledge and authority of the teacher to one in which the agency of students and teachers become more evenly balanced. Dadier achieved a modicum of success by bringing his students into the educational process by engaging with their interests in popular culture, music, and movies. While the 16 mm projector may no longer represent the cutting edge in visual education, the social interactions depicted in *Blackboard Jungle* between teacher, student, and screen remain relevant regardless of the changes that have taken place in the technological development of the media involved.

Fundamentally, the mode of the teacher augmented relies on screens and machines to realign the political, social, and cultural norms that have previously determined the power relations inherent in the discourse of pedagogy. Consequently, the shifts in agency and power brought about by the use of media technologies in the daily experience of surfing the Web or playing videogames (in addition to the more obvious instructional uses to which technology has been used in schools), suggests to linguist James Paul Gee in his research on the learning potential of electronic gaming that a structural relationship exists between learners and their tools (Adrian is one of Gee's research subjects):

> Adrian's knowledge and skills are not only distributed across himself and other people; some actually reside in various tools and technologies, like

the hex editors he can use to manipulate the code of a game. The knowledge built into the hex editor counts as Adrian's knowledge because he knows how to leverage this tool. The real thinking and acting unit becomes "Adrian plus tool."[43]

If "Adrian plus tool" is broadened to include teachers in addition to students, then the mode of the teacher augmented serves as a tripartite figure with which to compose teacher-student-screen as a relational unit. And depending on one's investment in current models of public education, the most realized form of the teacher augmented is also the most disorienting for traditional notions of what constitutes the pedagogical exchange. By moving pedagogy from a form relying on the teacher's body as focal point of instruction to one which immerses students into a visual matrix of process-based instruction centered on the notion of student plus tool. As educational researchers Jean Lave and Etienne Wenger suggest:

> A theory of social practice emphasizes the relational interdependency of agent and world, activity, meaning, cognition, learning, and knowing. It emphasizes the inherently socially negotiated character of meaning and the interested, concerned character of the thought and action of persons-in-activity. This view also claims that learning, thinking, and knowing are relations among people in activity in, with, and arising from the socially and culturally structured world.[44]

Immersive education—apprenticeships as suggested by Lave and Wenger, or simulations as I will suggest in a later chapter—disorients traditional pedagogical agents by displacing their authority and livelihood as dispensers of knowledge.[45] Therefore the teacher-augmented mode suggests radical changes in the foundation upon which traditional forms of education are built (and which can be situated clearly within the historical framework provided by progressive education and critical pedagogy). The teacher augmented will be more extensively examined in chapter 4 through a focus on the unstable power relations that developed during the production of *Trauber TV* (already intermittently discussed in relation to Dadier's tribulations in chapter 1), the daily student-produced television program that I supervised as a media production teacher during the 1990s.

The Teacher Embodied: The Screen as the Teacher

The final mode of pedagogical agency, the teacher embodied, returns the screen to its role as the primary teaching interface (at least superficially mirroring the mode of the teacher presented), but instead of simply representing the teacher on the screen it incorporates the cognitive, affective, and relational qualities of the flesh-and-blood teacher within the screen. The human–machine interaction upon which this mode depends can be implemented as simple forms of routine instruction through reinforcement as in the "teaching machines" envisioned by B. F. Skinner or as complex forms of structured instruction through simulation scenarios and immersive reality games which are being developed through a variety of research initiatives associated with AI, computer science, and new media (and are suggested by the research carried out by Gee).[46]

As evocative as these more complex forms of embodied teaching may seem, immersive reality and simulations build upon the two modes of pedagogical agency already described as presented and augmented. If the teacher-presented mode best represents the traditional lecture method of instruction and the teacher-augmented mode best represents the student-centered pedagogy of progressive education, then the teacher-embodied mode potentially reclaims older forms of instruction associated with seminars and the Socratic method (albeit transformed through the medium specific conditions associated with digital cinema, animation, and videogames). The remediation of the blackboard becomes the remediation of the teacher as the beloved teacher becomes content for the teacher-embodied mode of pedagogical agency as the blackboard had become content for the screens of educational media.

But, the particular teaching method (lecture, discussion, projects) used during the teacher-embodied mode of instruction is secondary to the necessity that there be a reciprocal interaction between a teaching machine/screen and a student. The pedagogical agent as teaching machine simulates the attentiveness of the flesh-and-blood teacher by providing engaging responses to student queries during instruction or training. In the most advanced systems, the instructional mechanism of the teaching machine also responds to the affective quality, not just the cognitive aspects, of the student. But as with the teacher presented and the teacher augmented, the teacher embodied represents a form of mediated-instruction with a history.

Television programs as disparate as *Winky-Dink and You* (1953–1957) and *Pee-wee's Playhouse* (1986–1990), both of which aired on CBS, provided viewers with, albeit quite simple, forms of interactivity, which seemed appropriate as formal approaches to engaging easily distracted children during Saturday morning television programming. *Winky-Dink and You* depended upon the use of a Mylar sheet to cover the television screen so that kids could use colored markers to draw directly onto the screen in response to cues provided by the show's narrative. Most of these cues were structured around the spectacle of movement—a typical segment featured Mike McBean (a recurring character) climbing up a ladder drawn by kids at the prodding of Jack Barry, the program's host: "Hurry Kids! Draw a ladder. Mike needs a ladder to escape!" While not particularly educational, other than to reinforce following directions and using the imagination to depict simple objects, *Winky-Dink* did explore, albeit primitively, forms of interaction with the screen in the context of the domestic sphere.

Similarly, *Pee-wee's Playhouse* usually included an opening sequence in which Pee-wee Herman, who served as the show's host, revealed the word of the day and instructed young viewers to scream whenever the word was said on that day's program. When the work was uttered, recurring characters such as Cowboy Curtis (Laurence Fishburne) and Conky the Robot began screaming as a montage of zooms and swish pans created a mild form of visual chaos onscreen. The word was then reinforced—spelling through text appearing onscreen and pronunciation through verbal repetition by key characters in the show—accompanied by a simple form of interaction (scream competitions and laughter usually followed in the setting that I watched Pee-wee in during the late 1980s—a hip show to watch in art school). The interactivity available on these programs was simplistic (determined to a great extent by the broadcast technologies of television) relying on characters instructing the viewer to act in relation to the screen—draw or scream—but the interaction did provide a motivating link to the program and its instructional contents. Both programs used interactivity as a form of extended entertainment which meant to encourage viewer loyalty (and in Pee-wee's case, done with a knowing tongue-in-cheek homage to earlier programs like *Winky-Dink*). As such, both programs provide a glimpse at early forays into the use of the teacher-embodied mode as represented by a screen through which a response is expected on the part of the viewer (in this case, children) and suggest the charismatic tone that defines the beloved teacher within the embodied mode—Jack Barry and Winky Dink as onscreen pals and Pee-wee as a maniacal friend and demented uncle figure in the guise of mentor.

The teacher-embodied mode of pedagogical agency will be examined in more detail in chapter 5 which focuses on several iterations of the STEVE virtual human training system developed by the U.S. Army during the first decade of the twenty-first century.

3

FRENCH IN ACTION

The Teacher Presented

The fact is ... if you want to use television for teaching somebody something, you have first to teach somebody how to use television. In this sense, television is not so different from a book. You can use books to teach, but first you must teach people about books, at least about alphabet and words, and then about levels of credibility, suspension of disbelief, the difference between a novel and a book on history and so on and so forth. In reality, I wonder whether there is a real difference between teaching people to read books and using books to teach people.

—Umberto Eco, "Can Television Teach?"[1]

I first encountered *French in Action* during its initial run in 1987 on WTTW, the Public Broadcasting Service (PBS) station in Chicago. The show, a college level telecourse on French language and culture, seemed ubiquitous. Midday or late night, whenever I switched on my small black-and-white television, there was an episode of *French in Action*. In stark contrast to the staid educational programming of the 1960s and 1970s, which often featured buttoned-down teachers droning woodenly before a blackboard, *French in Action* featured location footage shot in Paris, a large cast of characters (ranging from belligerent jerks to a mime), and clips from French film and television dramas and comedies. The two principal characters, Mireille and Robert, played out a faux romantic narrative with a strutting *jouissance* matched only by the charisma of Professor Pierre Capretz, the program's creator, as he presided over the instruction embedded in each episode. And many of the program's narrative vignettes seemed to evoke classic and New Wave French cinema with a wink and nod to the viewer in the know. Here was a telecourse that marked itself through substantial production technique, a colorful mis-en-scène, and a witty authorial voice.

As *Blackboard Jungle* provided a template for understanding the teacher-presented mode of pedagogical agency in its guise as a fictional representation of a teacher on the screen, *French in Action* provides the exemplar for the teacher-presented mode as an onscreen teacher delivering instruction directly to the viewer. In what follows, *French in Action* will be examined as a text that is intended to provide pedagogical content to a distant, unseen audience of students, mediated through the historical cultural form of the telecourse and authored by a professor. The teacher-presented mode situates the onscreen instructor as the bearer of pedagogy and often replaces the flesh-and-blood teacher entirely. But, as the ethnographic narratives that conclude this chapter indicate, Capretz's telecourse has a place, slipping from one category to another, within the teacher-augmented mode as it became a teaching tool for professors in language instruction courses at Yale University's French Department.

The Professor as Auteur

Pierre Capretz joined Yale as a French language instructor in the late 1950s. According to Capretz, following the launch of Sputnik in 1957, "lots of money became available" for "young mavericks" who sought to develop innovative teaching materials for courses in math, physics, and foreign languages.[2] Working with the federal government from 1958 through 1963, Capretz and a team of foreign language educators designed "daily life dialogues," short audio recordings of native speakers in conversation, which were used to train students in French, German, Russian, and Spanish. The instructional format of these taped dialogues challenged conventional approaches to language instruction as most materials used at the time depended on grammar and drill. Capretz's design team, by his own admission, "didn't know what we were doing," so they experimented by developing a number of modules using the dialogue format over several summer institutes aimed at secondary teachers throughout the United States. Capretz emphasized that he saw the work that he and his colleagues had accomplished as only "a beginning" toward improved methods for language instruction spurred on by the feverish climate of educational innovation following Sputnik. But working on these tape-based dialogues sparked his interest in using technology as an integrated component of classroom-based language instruction and led him to seek other outlets for his inventiveness in this area.

In 1962, in an attempt to foster new teaching methods amongst the faculty (and following a vogue for Skinner-type teaching machines), Yale purchased a "phonetics machine." Capretz, by his account being the only faculty member willing to learn to operate the machine, was asked to oversee its use in the curriculum. As he began employing the device in his already existing courses, his reputation as a technology leader in the Yale French Department grew. Emboldened by his success using the phonetics machine as a teaching tool,

Capretz experimented with creating simple multimedia presentations for his classes which incorporated French language audiovisual materials. He recorded himself reading a short story in French and played the tape for his class while projecting slide images onto dual side-by-side screens. These images illustrated the language being spoken on the audiotape and helped students to comprehend syntax, grammar, and meaning through a visual approach in contrast to the traditionally aural method used in most colleges. As he developed additional multimedia presentations he began to explore the relationship between the spoken French language text and the images that appeared on the screens. In our interview, he stressed that he conceived of the images and text as integral to his instructional approach, but also sought, using the media as a motivational tool, to entertain his students while teaching them French. His slide shows proved popular with students and his class enrollments subsequently mushroomed over the next few years.

He originally synchronized slide images with audio through the use of a "beep" sound similar to that used with classroom filmstrips at the time. While this method of integrating image and sound gave the feel of time-based media, it failed to provide the effect of full motion, so Capretz started renting 16 mm versions of his favorite French films to include in his presentations. Around this time he negotiated the rights to screen François Truffaut's *Jules et Jim* as part of his instructional content. Capretz continued to develop his approach to incorporating media into his instruction using a combination of film clips, photographs, art, voice, sound, and music throughout the 1970s. As he began in the early 1980s to write and design the *French in Action* telecourse (funded by the PBS affiliate WGBH in Boston), Capretz incorporated much of what he had learned from his use of media in his Yale courses.

As part of the ongoing educational programming produced for PBS, *French in Action* drew not only on Capretz's classroom experience but also on PBS programming that successfully integrated instructional content with the style of entertainment television shows. This combination of education and entertainment had been a topic of contention in the formation of PBS for the twenty years that preceded the production of Capretz's program. Congress authorized funding for PBS in 1967, pulling together stations that had been organized around a loosely knit alliance of educational and not-for-profit broadcasters.[3] At the time there was considerable debate around how much "educational" programming should figure into the regular schedule of PBS. In the end, a mandate for public interest programming with a generalized educational (read enrichment) intent won out as the characteristic programming to be aired by PBS affiliates. The program with the most explicitly educational agenda deemed a success by both viewers and critics was *Sesame Street*, first aired in 1969. *Sesame Street* provided preschool (and older) viewers with a balanced mix of entertainment and educational content. Never too didactic and always marbled throughout with high quality production value, this entertainment-educational format became the signature style of *Sesame Street* and to a large extent much of the explicitly educational programming on American public broadcasting.[4]

Another program format that proved to be successful during the early days of PBS was the multiepisode documentary (often imported from the UK) featuring a celebrity professor-host. Documentary series of this kind focused on topics central to traditional higher education with titles that often provided the viewer with what Matthew Arnold had referred to as the best that Western Civilization had to offer: *Civilisation* (a history of Western art and culture) with Sir Kenneth Clark (BBC, 1969), *Ways of Seeing* (an exploration of visual art) with John Berger (BBC, 1972),[5] and *The Ascent of Man* (a history of Western science) with Jacob Bronowski (BBC, 1973). By far the most popular of these productions has been *Cosmos,* hosted by the late Cornell astronomer, Carl Sagan (PBS, 1980). All of these programs depend on the onscreen charisma of their teacher-hosts. Sagan with his "billions and billions" refrain, parodied endlessly at the time by standup comics, provided viewers with an idiosyncratic and deeply knowledgeable guide through the subject of astronomy. The pedagogy enacted on screen in these programs flows through the figures of the celebrity expert-hosts as they jump from one heritage/art location to another and through their distinctive voices as each host provides voiceover for their respective series. In this case, the traditional voice of the documentary, as defined by film historian Bill Nichols as the voice that marks the authorial presence of expertise, is coincident with the voice of the onscreen host.[6]

The success of this celebrity-based form of instruction confirms educational historian James Zigerell's notion regarding the effectiveness of telecourses: "The better programs were not so much TV programs as they were simulated and enhanced classroom lectures, and always under the control of a visible professor. If the professor was articulate, warm, and at ease in the studio, so much the better for viewers."[7] Of course, for Sagan the classroom was the whole of the universe, while for Clark and Bronowski it was the length of recorded history in the West. All of these programs provided the "visible professor" with an "enhanced classroom," real when on location in a remote part of the world and virtual in the case of Sagan's famous calendar of the universe in which recorded human time is merely the last few seconds of the last day of the last month.

Each of the professor-hosts served as the onscreen performer, but also as the writer of the series in which they were featured. As has been recently noted in the case of Clark's *Civilisation*, each of the hosts exerted considerable influence over the day-to-day production of the programs and was directly involved in the selection of locations and the visualization of the scripts by camera operators and directors.[8] They became professor-auteurs as much as they were the presentational face of onscreen pedagogy. Capretz took this lineage and sought to make his mark on it as he began working on his own telecourse for PBS.

The Capretz Method: L'Histoire

The *French in Action* telecourse consists of fifty-two half-hour video programs, twenty-six audiotapes, two textbooks, two workbooks, and two study guides.[9] The first episode (*Leçon* 1) provides students with an overview of the material to follow, an explanation of the narrative and the characters that guide instruction, and an introduction to the pedagogical methods used throughout the run of the course. This initial lesson is delivered for the most part in English, but the student is warned that this is the last English language communication to be used in the series. *Leçon* 2 begins the process of instruction by using what Capretz describes onscreen in the previous lesson as the technique of "immersion."

Immersion allows students to "live" in a French-speaking environment for the duration of each individual episode and relies on a methodology that Capretz suggests follows the language acquisition approach seemingly innate to humans. Capretz explained that his immersion method mimics the manner in which a "baby learns ... little by little they pick up the language." It is important to note, though, that language researchers Ellen Bialystock and Kenji Hakuta in their overview of research on second-language acquisition dispute the notion that there is a "natural" way to learn a language, and Capretz acknowledges that his immersive approach to language instruction is based on "gut instinct" and not empirical research.[10] Nevertheless, for Capretz's method of immersion instruction, each French word is spoken several times by native French speakers during the course of an episode, and each instance of a given word is illustrated by actions and objects drawn from the *French in Action* narrative as well as from French magazines, film, and television. As all instruction and character interaction is given in French, there is no translation provided for the student. Students wholly new to the French language are likely, by Capretz's own admission, to become frustrated by their lack of comprehension, but Capretz assures the viewer that this is normal and in time will pass. Capretz states in the first episode: "French is French. It is not coded English. It does not work to translate." These are the last words that Capretz speaks in English.

As Rick Altman emphasized in his book on using video to teach foreign languages (written roughly contemporaneously with Capretz's program): "The Golden Rule of video pedagogy, a rule that should be remembered every day and every hour, would be: *Don't expect—or even seek—full comprehension.*"[11] Capretz follows this "golden rule" in his pedagogical method, but to minimize early periods of learner confusion, he suggests four techniques, repeated throughout the English language instruction in the first episode, to use while learning through the "Capretz Method:" "observe, imitate, speak out, and practice." Capretz gives these commands to the viewer in a friendly yet emphatic tone meant to invoke a ritualized response when viewers are asked to verbally address Capretz or other characters within the tape. At intervals throughout each program, specific words and phrases are repeated through a replay of the

FIGURE 3.1 The blackboard remediated. *French in Action* (WGBH-TV, Wellesley College, and Yale University, 1987)

video material—sometimes twice, sometimes more. Once during each individual program a shot-reverse shot sequence is used to encourage the viewer to repeat what a character has just said over a freeze frame of that same character speaking the phrase.[12] These interactive "speak out" moments fail, as the pause is too short, giving the viewer little time to respond, a pacing flaw that Capretz acknowledged during our interview.[13]

Each episode of *French in Action* constitutes a lesson, and each lesson begins with an installment of the ongoing story that forms the core of the series. At the conclusion of each episode's story, which lasts on average six minutes, there is a zoom-out, zoom-in transition to a full-frame image of Professor Capretz sitting at a podium with a green chalkboard as the background. The remainder of the tape provides students with instruction from Capretz as the teacher figure onscreen and as the voiceover narrator of the material illustrating French words and phrases. The instructional portion is composed of the following discrete elements: interviews with native French speakers on the streets of Paris; excerpts from French cinema and television (comedic and dramatic series and commercials) that illustrate French language and culture (including body language—emphasized throughout the course as particularly important to French communication style); cartoons (which give the viewer a glimpse into the specificity of French humor); and printed materials (which place the viewer inside the "French cultural system").

The ongoing story which begins each lesson, "*l'histoire*," as Capretz calls it, features two principal characters: a young French woman, Mireille, and a young American man, Robert. Mireille comes from a middle-class extended family living in Paris, and Robert is the product of an American East Coast single parent family (his father and mother having divorced when Robert was young). During the first ten episodes, the opening narrative segment focuses on Capretz as he teaches his French class at Yale (he greets his students as they enter the classroom and asks them their names and inquires about their favorite type of movies and books). He introduces the idea that the class will be creating a story so as to more pleasurably learn to speak French. There is some humor provided by one student who enjoys contradicting whatever Capretz suggests regarding the communal creation of the story. "Should the man be Norwegian?" asks Capretz (hinting that he would like the male protagonist to be American). "Yes!" responds the annoying student. "No!" exclaims Capretz good naturedly as he signals his disapproval with a swipe of his outstretched arm.

Over the first ten episodes the story begins to take shape as the students, with the helpful (and pedagogical) oversight of Professor Capretz, construct a narrative from which to gain proficiency in the French language. The resulting story has Mireille as a blue eyed blond and Robert as brunette and healthy—"*ça va!*" Mireille, over the course of the series, develops a relationship with Robert

FIGURE 3.2 Students assist in constructing l'histoire. *French in Action* (WGBH-TV, Wellesley College, and Yale University, 1987)

while attending school, spends considerable time reading in the Luxembourg Garden, and interacts with family and friends over meals at home and drinks at the café. All of these characters and locations allow ample opportunity for French language and culture to be explored while providing students with amusing stories and situations in order to facilitate a more enjoyable approach to learning a new language.

The actual instruction in the tape develops from the interplay between the storyline featuring Mireille and Robert and the direct instruction provided by Professor Capretz. The narrative operates as a motivational element within the tape, with the instruction parsed in relation to the amount of new material contained within the body of the story. The story is light-hearted and repetitive for easy retention, and it relies on stereotypes to quickly telegraph the intentions and meanings of character interactions.[14] All of the classic, one might say clichéd, French national characters appear: Jean-Claude (the mime), Aunt Georgette (the addled relative), Hubert (the overeager college friend), and Ousmane (the urbane, intelligent postcolonial subject). These are only a few of the large cast of characters that populate the Paris of *French in Action*, but they are representative.

Interestingly, Capretz is not the only professor figure represented within the program. A marginal but recurring figure in the ongoing narrative is the art history professor, and his image is one of a befuddled older academic possibly smitten with his erstwhile student, Mireille. This second professor embodies the popular idea of the ivory tower eccentric who exhibits poor social skills and a severe disconnect from daily life. Media theorist Jostein Gripsrud suggests that popular representations of the academic follow two main forms:

> The centuries (if not millennia)-old opposition between the stereotypes of "the bookworm" and "the experienced person" is then worth keeping in mind when looking at how academics and other intellectuals appear on television. Such stereotypes are condensations of a number of more specific character traits, which in this case could be grouped in oppositional pairs such as weak v. strong, feminine v. masculine, timid v. self-confident.... It is not difficult to imagine how physical appearance and body language may be used to categorize many traditional academics.[15]

Within the overarching narrative of *French in Action* (the metanarrative that contains both the storyline and the direct instruction) Capretz figures as the second of Gripsrud's academics, "the experienced person," while the art history professor, identified by his occupation as much as by his behavior, figures as the other character, "the bookworm." Capretz is the author of the text. Capretz is the interlocutor. Capretz is the narrative voice of the program by virtue of his dual role as host/professor and as voiceover. In contrast, the art history "professor" is merely a bookworm: "powerless and sexless," absentminded and socially inept.[16]

FIGURE 3.3 Pierre Capretz as the Professor. *French in Action* (WGBH-TV, Wellesley College, and Yale University, 1987)

In his role as professor-figure and televisual auteur, Pierre Capretz thus brings to fruition the role of the onscreen instructor that once made early educational television possible, while providing it with a more aesthetically energetic style. Capretz marries the charisma of a Harvey White (the physics professor featured on NBC's *Continental Classroom*) with the celebrity gestures of Bronowski and Sagan (famous professors who were also entertainers) while deploying the stereotype of the professor for its use as a pedagogical device. This tension between the telegenic professor and the characteristically desexed and ineffectual "professor" is symptomatic of only one of the many problematic stereotypical depictions of class and gender interests upon which the program trades, and these issues will be taken up further in the next section.[17]

In addition to the characters who inhabit the narrative, Capretz himself enters the main story from time to time. An example of this blending of motivational storyline and instructional technique is a scene in which Professor Capretz, in direct address to the camera, says, "Merci." This is followed by a long montage sequence of people from film and television, as well as characters from within the *French in Action* storyline, saying *merci* in a variety of situations: *Merci, merci, merci.* Finally, the program cuts back to Capretz who gestures off camera followed by a cut to a woman sitting on a park bench. Capretz enters the scene, picks up a coin that lies on the ground in front of the woman and offers it to her. She smiles appreciatively and takes the coin from Capretz. She says, "Merci." He exits the frame. Cut back to the classroom. Capretz enters the frame, sits down, and smiles broadly while gesturing with his hands: "Voilà." This self-reflexive moment allows Capretz to be simultaneously the author of the instructional curriculum, the teacher of the instructional instance (the teacher presented in terms of pedagogical agency), and the teacher figure in the instructional narrative. Capretz, the teacher-auteur, provides the learner-viewer with a model for interaction with the instructional method embedded within the program. The learner-viewer inhabits a character role for him- or herself; a role with which to interact with the screen.

In fact, the program's reliance on scenes depicting school and family, obviously in an attempt to situate the majority of viewers in familiar settings, suggests Bourdieu's notion that "academic capital is in fact the guaranteed product of the combined effects of cultural transmission by the family and cultural transmission by the school (the efficiency of which depends on the amount of cultural capital directly inherited from the family)."[18] As the subjects addressed by Capretz are students—within the narrative as he speaks to his class and within the real world as the tape plays—this representation of a family and school dominated by middle- and upper-class French values (or at least American ideas of such) provides viewers with a potentially overdetermined set of narrative codes. The student-subject is at once a student of the French language and culture in the pure pedagogical sense and also a potential consumer of French language and culture in the form of tourism. There is an implied conclusion that like the American student Robert, one day the viewer of *French in Action* will travel to France, take in the sights and sounds of Paris, and perhaps fall in love.

Tourist Pedagogy and the Consumption of Frenchness

Sociologist John Urry theorizes the visual culture of tourism as a form of everyday semiosis:

> There is the seeing of particular signs, such as the typical English village, the typical American skyscraper, the typical German beer-garden, the typical French château, and so on. This mode of gazing shows how tourists are in a way semioticians, reading the landscape for signifiers of certain pre-established notions or signs derived from various discourses of travel and tourism.[19]

The tourist collects signs (postcards, snapshots, and tchotchkes) which are littered throughout the landscape, commercial and natural, of his or her travels to exotic locales. The semiotician does his or her collecting in a self-conscious manner, but the tourist does so as a matter of habit. As a tourist in training, the student of a foreign language collects words, phrases, and syntax in order to attain fluency in cultural norms. This acquisition of language is itself a first step in the creation of a comfortably consumable object, in this case French culture.

French, to Americans, is a luxury language. Whereas one's rationale for studying Japanese may be due to its utility as a "business" language (especially during the economic bubble of the 1980s and the dot.com boom of the 1990s) or for studying Spanish may be due to its usefulness within economies highly dependent upon labor and goods from Mexico and Latin America (as is the case in Los Angeles and Southern California) one wishes to learn French, the quintessential "romance" language, so that one can travel to France to consume "Frenchness." And this desire is not only evident throughout the *French in Action* telecourse, it also structures the curriculum of *French in Action* around tourism and the markers of being French.

What is Frenchness? It is, in short, a culturally constructed identity situated for consumption by tourists that has been constructed by French society as a signifier of nationality and as a commodity for export.[20] This is not to make a qualitative judgment regarding Frenchness, or tourism for that matter, as both should be seen in the context of this study as explanatory concepts and not simply as reflexive critical concepts from which to deride the French culture industry or Capretz's telecourse. As sociologist Dean MacCannell says, "The modern critique of tourists is not an analytical reflection on the problem of tourism—it is part of the problem. Tourists are not criticized by [Daniel] Boorstin and others for leaving home to see sights. They are reproached for being satisfied with superficial experiences of other peoples and other places."[21] And this is exactly what Capretz tries to avoid: he tries to provide an in-depth experience of France and French language and culture for his viewers. Of course, as he is bound up with a postwar notion of Frenchness deriving from French art photography and New Wave cinema as much as from the lineage of traditional foreign language textbooks, his program by extension presents troubling aspects of identity to the viewer.

Nevertheless, both concepts, tourism and Frenchness, are presented here as a way to understand how the *French in Action* telecourse constructs an object of knowledge—French language and culture—using a narrative grounded in cinematic forms of discourse. Peter Hamilton, in his article on French postwar humanist photography, describes the visual aspects of Frenchness in the 1950s:

> In the typical representations of Frenchness which appear in the work of humanist photographers [Henri Cartier-Bresson, Robert Doisneau, and Willy Ronis], a new consensus about French society and about what it means to have a French identity is in the process of being forged. It is built around certain key themes or "sites"—*la rue* (the street); children and play; the family; love and lovers; Paris and its sights; *clochards* (homeless and marginal characters); *fêtes populaires* (fairs and celebrations); *bistros; habitations* (housing and housing conditions); work and craft. Representations of these themes served to reconstruct Frenchness as a unifying

identity in a period of major social, political, economic, and cultural change.[22]

Subject matter of French national identity—the street, children and play, the family, love and lovers, Paris and its sights—are replayed in countless postwar photographs in addition to many of the films of the French New Wave. If one watches even a few episodes of *French in Action*, one sees many of the characteristic images of postwar humanist photography. Robert and Mireille travel through the streets meeting and greeting the common, and at times not so common, folk with the sights of Paris and the French countryside as a backdrop to their adventures. Many of Mireille's and Robert's friends are students at the Sorbonne who will seem familiar to the students who sit in class and watch the telecourse as part of their instruction. Marie-Laure, Mireille's precocious little sister, figures prominently in many of the scenes; for example she sails her boat as Robert and Mireille flirt in the Luxembourg Garden. Robert is himself a tourist, having recently arrived in France (or so goes the storyline constructed by Capretz and his onscreen students).

The opening and ending credits of *French in Action* scroll across location shots of Paris that call to mind video footage from a travelogue. Throughout the program, each time that Capretz admonishes students to learn to speak French or to say a word or phrase in French, a kinetic sculpture by Niki de Saint Phalle and Jean Tinguely in the Stravinsky fountain at the Centre Pompidou appears onscreen to coincide with Capretz's command. Saint Phalle and Tinguely's sculpture features huge red lips that gyrate up and down as the machinery rotates. "Parlez Français," says Capretz. As is typical in foreign language instructional materials, reasons that contort the logic of the storyline are given for the characters to travel throughout the city (Robert takes the wrong Metro train, protesting students divert Mireille, a mysterious man spies on both of them).

After a brief digression (lessons 10 and 11) in which we find Mireille and her relatives stuck in a cabin during a vacation to Brittany, the narrative proper—*l'histoire*—begins with the arrival of Robert in present day Paris (circa 1986) at the De Gaulle Airport. He takes a taxi to the Latin Quarter and over the next several episodes spends time sightseeing (allowing for instructional time dedicated to location and customs of modern France). Meanwhile, Mireille sits reading in the Luxembourg Garden. She is briefly flirted with by Jean-Pierre, the failed pick-up artist, and then walks to the Sorbonne to attend art history class. On the way she is blocked by a group of protesting students who have already diverted Robert from his sightseeing. The two principal *French in Action* characters finally meet one another in lesson 14 and they exchange smiles. Romance is in the air.

The trajectory of this storyline, with each of its cluster of topics, moves from the classroom setting to the streets of Paris, with Robert and Mireille at the center of the narrative and Capretz at the center of instruction. Capretz's method

qu'est-ce que vous faites?

FIGURE 3.4 Mireille (Valérie Allain) and Robert (Charles Mayer) in Paris. *French in Action* (WGBH-TV, Wellesley College, and Yale University, 1987)

of directly addressing his class of fictional students changes into a mostly third person narrative mode beginning with lessons 10 and 11. Each of the changes in the narrative, from Capretz's fictional classroom to the Brittany vacation to Robert and Mireille's initial meeting, signifies a change in the linguistic mode of interaction. Students are first guided through basic words and phrases by the onscreen professor, and then introduced to longer sentences concerning pick-up artists and art history. From lesson 15 to 19 a model of conversational communication is presented through an extended dialogue between Mireille and Robert as they sip wine at a sidewalk café following their agreeable exchange on the street.

Our time spent in the Luxembourg Garden, within the narrative, provides us, the student-viewers, with examples of the scenic beauty of urban Paris as well as with a variety of situations that evoke the imagery of the humanist photographers examined in Hamilton's article—child and boat, love and lovers, the sights of Paris and such—while teaching us more complicated sentences. But each of these scenes also evokes Capretz's love of the French New Wave, in particular the film *Jules et Jim* which has already been mentioned as structuring early versions of his classroom instruction. Throughout *French in Action* there are moments that call to mind classic scenes from the films of Truffaut and Godard in their locations and subject matter. During our interview

Capretz invoked the names of Godard, Truffaut, Resnais, and Rouch several times while explaining the visual style of his telecourse; although he never discussed their direct influence on his creation of *French in Action*, he did speak of the style of his favorite films as an inspiration in the writing and directing of his program. Regardless, the implicit assumption of the visual and narrative content of *French in Action* is that the French language learner is a lover—of French cinema and of travel to Paris.[23]

Observing *French in Action* at Yale

As the onscreen professor in *French in Action*, Pierre Capretz, shock of white hair and distinguished aquiline features, represents the teacher presented from a programmatic perspective. The flesh-and-blood Pierre Capretz who sits in the audience at a Yale University French class as his colleagues use *French in Action* to instruct students on the intricacies of French language and culture, however, moves into the realm of the teacher-augmented mode of pedagogical agency. This move from one mode to another, a blurring of the distinctions between the modes of presentation and augmentation, highlights the complex fluctuations that account for mediated pedagogy and undercuts clearly marked boundaries between any of the three categories of pedagogical agency (signaling the interactivity associated with each participant within a given mode). The trending toward one mode or another makes the categories definable, the blurring at the edges makes them potentially more durable.

Presentation Session: Leçons 22 and 23

Sandra Lindstrom stands before a large projected video image. On screen, frozen midsentence, is Professor Pierre Capretz. Seated beside me in the darkened language lab is Professor Capretz in the flesh. Occasionally, students participating in that day's instruction, based on leçons 22 and 23 of *French in Action,* glance back at the professor, some startled at seeing *le professeur* in person and others comparing his image on the screen to his actual appearance nearly twenty years later. Capretz graciously smiles at the students while listening intently to Ms. Lindstrom as she guides her class through the material presented by the figure of Professor Capretz on screen.[24]

Ms. Lindstrom, a lecturer in the French Department at Yale, uses a handheld touch-screen remote control to fast forward through this day's program. Professor Capretz, Mireille, Robert, and the other characters in *l'histoire* move past at a comically accelerated pace. Lindstrom pauses the disk again to make a comment on the scene which students have just seen played out before them. She begins the lesson, which is delivered entirely in French, by screening the opening narrative section of Leçon 22.[25] Robert attempts to phone Madame Courtois but finds it difficult to understand the cultural norms attending to phones in Paris. Fortunately, a friendly Parisian comes to his aid and explains that to make a call on a public phone one must use a "telecarte," a prepaid phone card. Robert completes his call and accepts an invitation to dine with Madame Courtois and her husband later that evening.

At this point, Capretz appears on screen and begins the instructional portion of the *French in Action* program. Lindstrom moves about the class using the touch-screen remote to jump the laser disk to different parts of the program for illustration and review as she rapidly asks questions, repeats key phrases, and engages in brief conversations with her students. Lindstrom's classroom interactions follow the sequence of onscreen instructional materials provided by Capretz's telecourse. The video displayed on a large plasma screen monitor in the front of the classroom is clear, bright, and sharp.

Each student in the class sits at a computer workstation. The wood tables are divided into carrels with a large computer monitor sunken at a forty-five degree angle into the surface of the desk. A keyboard and mouse are stored for easy access on a swivel drawer beneath the surface of the table. Each of the computers is mounted with an antiglare screen and includes a set of headphones and a microphone for audio-based assignments. The room itself is a former library converted into its current layout as a computer lab. The walls are deeply stained wood with an antique patina that suggests the kind of august past that is often associated with Ivy League universities.

About thirty minutes into the fifty-minute class session, the touch-screen remote stops working. Lindstrom calmly continues to ask questions as she walks over to a locked wall cabinet and removes a simpler, conventional remote. She continues to jump the disk to various scenes, but the replacement remote fails to do so as accurately as the touch-screen model. She walks back to the wall cabinet and swaps out the laser disk containing leçon 22 for that containing leçon 23. This time she truncates the narrative part of the tape (as she did in the previous lesson with Capretz's onscreen instructional material) fast-forwarding through sections that she summarizes for her students.

The conventional remote continues to give her trouble—it will not pause the disk abruptly at a frame unless she points it directly at the laser disk player. She masks the functional inadequacies of the remote by seamlessly continuing to question her students. Despite the technological interruptions, Capretz seems enthralled by her performance (or at least is generous in his collegial support). Capretz later tells me that each class meeting for French language courses focuses on two episodes from his telecourse. By doing so, the accelerated French language classes, entitled "intensive" within the curricular jargon of the Yale French Department, are able to move efficiently through all fifty-two episodes of the program by the end of a single school year. Students appear generally attentive to the program (although student attentiveness may simply reflect Capretz's presence in the room) and laugh at appropriate moments within the narrative.

Lindstrom relies on the humor and narrative fascination of the *French in Action* program to draw students into her instruction. She plays short segments, mostly phrases, and then encourages students to repeat the phrases aloud. Students have obviously been trained to interact with Lindstrom in this manner. Following Eco's notion that to use television as a pedagogical tool the use of the tool must be taught, the students seem to understand at this point in the school year, mid-January, what responses are expected of them during a *French in Action* class session. Of course, the typical anonymity of this form of entire class recital method allows many students to merely mouth the appearance of an appropriate response or remain silent. Due to time constraints and the number of students in class, any individual student can blend into the crowd during the call-and-response session. While the technology at Yale seemed superior to that available to the typical public school professor, Lindstrom follows the same practical instructional procedures that I had observed at other institutions.

Practice Session: Leçon 43

Later as we enter a tiny classroom in the basement of an older building on the Yale campus, Capretz explains to me that the student leading the practice session this morning is an exchange student, Michel, from the École Normale Supérieure in Paris. Michel stands at the front of the classroom holding the *French in Action* instructor's guide as he writes a set of French words in chalk on the blackboard. He engages in a call-and-response review session with six students gathered around a small steel conference table. He asks questions in French and then waits for the students to respond. For the most part, they stare blankly at him. When they fail to respond, he follows up with another question and eventually answers the question himself. At times he gestures with the instructor's guide or the chalk to encourage students to answer his queries. From time to time he turns to the blackboard and writes key terms or phrases to which students were introduced during the previous day's class session.

He seems slightly nervous, but it is difficult to tell whether he is caught off-guard by having visitors present during his session or if it is teaching itself that he finds unnerving. He stumbles over words and phrases in what appears to be an attempt to speak slowly so that his students will understand him. He sways back and forth on the balls of his feet and fidgets with the instructor's guide as he surveys the students for the appropriate responses. He begins writing a series of French words on the board and at one point writes "rationalité," "Descartes," and "Cartesien(ne)." He seems to think this will spark a series of connections for his students, but the students again fail to respond. As this is Yale, I assume that the reference did not pass them by, but nevertheless it did not have the effect Michel intended. A female student raises her hand and asks a question that takes several minutes for her to conclude. Michel seems stumped as he searches through his notes. He draws a figure on the board that resembles a wagon wheel and points to one of the spokes while commenting in French. Once again, none of the students respond. The class session ends. Professor Capretz and I thank Michel as we leave.

I am uncertain as to how representative this session is of practice sessions in general at Yale. I mention this to Capretz and, although I have been told by others in the French Department that the École Normale students are Capretz's "pet" students, he dismisses Michel's session with a wave of his hand. He emphasizes that Michel was a poor teacher and that this was not how he had intended for the practice sessions to be led. He promises to schedule me a visit to a classroom with a better prepared review section leader.

Presentation Session: Leçon 44

The following day, Capretz and I are seated in a room that serves as the French Department library and as a class screening room. Leather bound books line the walls, a large screen plasma television monitor dominates the front, video and audio equipment spills out from a closet near the entrance, and computer kiosks provide students with workstations akin to those installed in Ms. Lindstrom's room from the previous day's session. The workstations are shut down as about twenty students sit comfortably around a large wooden conference table. Capretz remarks as we survey the room, "Theoretically the practice session instructors should attend the presentations, but theory and practice...." He shrugs. Michel, the teaching assistant from the École Normale, is absent.

Alice Magden, the instructor for this session, introduces herself using strongly accented English, which I am unable to place, but regardless evokes my fondest cinematic fantasies of European culture and sophistication. She appears to be good friends with Capretz. He speaks highly of her teaching abilities and suggests that this session will make up for the poorly led practice session the day before. Capretz and I are seated at the back of the room: one student does a double take as he eyes the professor and stammers, "You're the guy in the videos." Capretz smiles and nods his head as several students giggle at their colleague's outburst (this must happen a lot).

Ms. Magden calls the class to order and begins screening a few seconds of the narrative portion of *French in Action*. She pauses the disk and rapidly throws out questions to her students. They respond as rapidly with answers that seem to satisfy her. She plays a few more seconds of the tape, pausing on a specific word. She rewinds and replays the word. She calls on a male student leaning back in his chair. He does not understand what is being said (in French, of course), and she jokes with him regarding his failure to comprehend. His fellow students laugh at the good natured interplay between Magden and her diffident student. She skips the laser disk forward what seems to be only a few frames and then plays a sentence of Capretz's pedagogical comments. She fires off more questions, carefully engaging with students who have not yet responded.

Magden navigates through *French in Action* using a touch-screen remote similar to the one used the day before by Lindstrom. Like Lindstrom, Magden is quite adept at stopping, starting, and jumping across the program in response to whatever word, phrase, or concept she is teaching. Unlike Lindstrom, Magden breaks the narrative and instructional material into microsegments, sometimes playing only a single utterance by a character on screen. She repeats this utterance verbally and then leads students in recitation until pronunciation is correct. On screen, Robert shops for shoes. In the classroom, Magden pauses the disk and jokes about the cowboy boots that Robert considers buying. The students laugh as she repeats the segment one more time.

European shoe sizes flash by on the screen as Robert attempts to figure out what size he should buy (the difference between American and European shoe sizes confuses him). At this point, as she tries to get students to answer questions about shoe size, Magden's interaction with the class begins to deteriorate somewhat. This seems to be new material for the students, so they are not responding as quickly as they had at the beginning of class. Magden responds patiently and with good humor at their awkward and incorrect answers. On the screen, Mireille and Aunt Georgette chat about Georgette's dog, Fido. Magden pauses the disk and replays the scene again. She breaks this scene down into micro-utterances as she had done with the scene involving Robert and the shoes. Abruptly, the touch-screen remote stops working. Magden calmly retrieves the conventional remote control from the equipment closet. Her students remain attentive during this momentary break in class (they have probably seen this happen before).

At this point, Magden begins what Capretz refers to as "reinvention of the story." She asks students to rework portions of the story using the elements provided by the telecourse, but to go further by including words and phrases learned during previous lessons. Magden reviews the dialogue between Mireille and Georgette concerning Fido and then returns to the scene with Robert and the shoes. She concludes her review by reminding students to attend their practice sessions and then dismisses class.

Practice Session: Leçons 22 and 23

Five students are present as a tall, young man dressed in a dark blue suit takes roll. Paul, a Yale graduate student, comes highly recommended by the French Department. He writes on the blackboard, as he counts along in French, the following sequence of numbers: 01, [43, 45, 72, 07] 06. A student arrives late, followed by two more. He greets the students enthusiastically as they enter, "Bonjour!"

Paul moves around the classroom questioning students about the numbers on the board. He repeats the numbers aloud several times emphasizing pronunciation on each try. Students who answer correctly, he congratulates. Those who answer incorrectly, he gently chides. The students seem to enjoy his teaching style, and he performs with gusto. He corrects pronunciation by repeating words and phrases used by students aloud as if in song. He gestures so as to sneak a clue to students as he awaits their correct answers. He gestures to his ear. Students laugh. He pauses, listening for a response, then snaps back into performance as he barks out an answer.

A female student enters late. Paul intones, "Ah, Madame," and smiles as he gestures to her chair. He makes eye contact with students as he crosses the front of the classroom. "Tres Bien!" "Bon!" He calls on each student while keeping the pace fast. He stops, momentarily allowing students to collect their thoughts, before he moves to the blackboard.

Paul draws a diagram on the board. He poses a question. No one responds, so he imitates a loud buzzer sound from a television game show. Students laugh. He explains that the drawing represents the places that Robert visits during his ride on the metro to Madame Courtois' apartment and then asks a follow-up question. Again students remain silent, so he mimes confusion and glances furtively about the classroom. He blurts out the buzzer noise again and then answers his own question.

I briefly nod off—the room is warm. I am caught dozing by a student who is glancing back at Capretz (again!). As I snap to attention, I notice that Paul has the instructor's guide open on his desk. He has not looked at it during the entire hour-long practice session, so it must serve as a safety net at those moments when he needs a reference during a session. Paul questions another student, who fails to understand, so Paul pulls out his wallet and begins to illustrate the correct answer using simple French words and the wallet as a prop. Students nod signaling comprehension and some respond with the appropriate verbal cue. Paul dismisses class and begins to pack up his materials. He remains to answer questions and to discuss instructional matters with a few students who linger about after class.

Presentation: The Staging of Pedagogical Narratives

Each episode of *French in Action* concludes with a short sequence staged as a traditional "Punch and Judy" puppet show attended by a group of school children. Puppet versions of Capretz's characters appear and interact with Punch, restating and reviewing material learned during the episode. At the end of one of these segments, Punch exits stage right and returns with a large board. He then whacks a character on its head (most often Robert's puppet double) thereby fulfilling his role as Punch. Cut to children laughing joyfully. The tiny curtains close on the puppet stage as Punch sticks his head out and displays a sign reading "Fin."

These concluding sequences featuring Punch self-consciously reference the representational nature of *French in Action*. They catch Capretz in the act of

FIGURE 3.5 Punch and Mireille on stage. *French in Action* (WGBH-TV, Wellesley College, and Yale University, 1987)

a creative version of throwing in everything-but-the-kitchen-sink—cinema, television, magazines, puppets, romance, scenic Paris, and a large cast of French national character types. This soup of narrative elements and cultural references reflects the pedagogical approach that Capretz developed in an ad hoc manner over the twenty years prior to beginning work on the *French in Action* episodes. As a cultural production utilizing the generic characteristics of a PBS style telecourse, *French in Action* exemplifies the teacher-presented mode of peda-gogical agency. Like the fictional figure of the teacher presented by Dadier and Escalante, Capretz appears onscreen as a narrative figure, but also as an agent of instruction (which trumps the Hollywood teachers who enact pedagogy merely as a plot point or to provide authenticity to a school-based narrative). *French in Action* is explicit in its instructional intent and uses the story and char-acters (and the *Nouvelle Vague* flourishes) as motivational and illustrative tools in the hands of the actual teacher on the screen: Pierre Capretz.

And as the teacher, Capretz exemplifies the professor-auteur: a combined media producer and educational designer, envisioned as simply a content pro-vider by administrators, that may be increasingly prominent as online and vir-tual forms of instruction begin to trouble the distinct separation that has existed between the design of courses and syllabi and the performance of pedagogy by professors. Consequently, in Capretz's program, the professor-auteur becomes synonymous with the teacher-figure as it becomes the teacher presented. But while these two roles, professor-auteur and teacher presented, can be linked, they can also be separated as the onscreen teacher merely designates an actor performing a narrative of pedagogy that has been written and directed by the professor-auteur (in Capretz's case). Regardless of the intricacies of the pedagogical act envisioned in the teacher-presented mode of pedagogical agency, the key component of this mode is that the teacher and screen become one and that the pedagogy flows one way: from teacher or professor on the screen to student in the audience.

For Capretz (as evidenced by his enthusiasm for them during our classroom observations), Ms. Magden and Ms. Lindstrom are outstanding representatives of the ways in which the *French in Action* program can be used in a classroom setting. Through their performative and entertaining pedagogy it is obvious why Capretz had resisted my initial attempts to exclusively categorize his work as a model of the teacher presented. While it remains true that the onscreen Capretz as a standalone instructional media figure does exemplify a literal manifestation of the teacher presented, the use of his program by his colleagues at Yale clearly represents the teacher-augmented mode as well. The circuit of instruction moves continuously between teacher, students, and media throughout the class session. The teacher in the classroom acts as a guide who directs student attention toward the currently "hot spot" of pedagogy in the classroom. The focal point of instruction still resides with the teacher, but throughout the session the pedagogical interaction moves from teacher, to student, to screen.

While Michel's review session was admittedly weak (and designated as such by Capretz), Paul's review session, while eschewing media as a specific part of instruction, transformed Capretz's ideas into an engaging student-centered educational performance. Although Paul remained the pedagogical focus throughout the session, he did at crucial points effortlessly transfer that focal point to his students in a way that brought laughter and engagement. While no televisual media were used during his class session, he relied on the blackboard throughout to illustrate points brought up by students. As in Michel's session, Paul's use of the blackboard as a visual reinforcement of instruction seemed to fail as an assist to students (they still seemed uncomprehending of the points he was attempting to make). But Paul compensated for the lack of explicitly visual material by relying on theatrical techniques to grab student attention and by referencing scenes and characters from the telecourse. He provided a narrative context for the material being presented and used the story from *French in Action* as his frame of reference for review.

These narrative, spatial, visual, and performative aspects of pedagogical agency signal the move from the two-dimensional screen representation of the teacher as a narrative character and instructional figure—ably exemplified first by Dadier and second by Capretz—to an engagement in the three-dimensional physical world with actual teachers and students. What distinguishes the teacher-augmented mode as unique in relation to the long history of education as seminar, lecture, and discussion is the introduction of media, technology, and screens into the space of education. This new configuration, which builds on the historical uses of the blackboard, changes up the relations between student and teacher, but also shifts the politics from one of assumed authority and earned experience to one dependent on distributed agency and diffused circles of power. This expanded notion of the interactive space of the classroom, seen as inherently liberating by proponents of critical pedagogy and progressive education, will be examined more explicitly in the examination of students as producers of media in the following chapter.

4

TRAUBER TV

The Teacher Augmented

Freud, as we know, practiced self-analysis. The question facing anthropologists today is how best to integrate the subjectivity of those they observe into their analysis: in other words, how to redefine the conditions of representativeness to take account of the renewed status of the individual in our societies. We cannot rule out the possibility that the anthropologist, following Freud's example, might care to consider himself as indigenous to his own culture—a privileged informant, so to speak—and risk a few attempts at ethno-self-analysis.

—Marc Augé, *Non-places*[1]

During most of my six years at John Trauber High School my day began with a flip of a switch. Every morning at the break between first and second periods, I activated television monitors throughout the school. The *Trauber TV* logo would pop on screen accompanied by music ranging from hip-hop to big band. As the bell rang signaling the start of class, two student hosts, sitting before cameras in the school's television studio, would appear onscreen and exclaim, "Good morning, John Trauber!"

This greeting, blurted out of speakers across campus, sought to grab the attention of the distracted and often sleepy students who sat at desks awaiting the beginning of class instruction time. It also signaled that they were about to hear the school bulletin and, if all went well, view a short feature segment highlighting events or personalities at Trauber High. As the segment concluded, the hosts would reappear and bid their fellow students, "Have a great day." End credits rolled as more music played. Another flip of the switch and television monitors went dark across the school.

This sketch represents an ideal version of what *Trauber TV* could be. Many days cues were missed, bulletin items were garbled, shots misframed or out of focus, and microphones or other equipment broken. On any given day many classrooms were unable to receive the show due to faulty wiring or damaged television sets. On several occasions the computer-based scheduler arbitrarily switched on television monitors in some parts of the school, and the *Oprah Winfrey Show* would abruptly appear and disappear while teachers were trying to teach. But regardless, and sometimes in the face of student disenchantment with the technical problems that seemed to overshadow their involvement in producing the program, *Trauber TV* went on every morning.

Technology at Trauber

John Trauber High School sits across the San Francisco bay from the region in Northern California known as Silicon Valley. Located in the city of Vista Valley, the school in the 1990s served a student population of over 4,200 students, of whom 26% were Latino, 24% Asian, 20% Caucasian, 18% Filipino, and 11% African American. The surrounding community, historically employing most of its citizens in agricultural jobs, underwent a dramatic shift during the mid-1990s, influenced largely by the transformation of the city into a bedroom community for high tech corporations located in Palo Alto and San Jose, and had become economically diverse as well. The Vista Valley Unified School District had a history of commitment to using media and technology in its classrooms beginning with the creation of a district wide technology plan in the late 1970s. In the fall of 1994, the district implemented a third version of the earlier technology plan financed through a multimillion dollar bond levy passed by Vista Valley voters the previous year. At the heart of the new plan was a promise to equip every classroom in the district with six Apple Macintosh computers and a laser printer. These computers were to be networked through high-speed fiber optics wired to the district's main server. In addition to this computer-based technology, the district installed a video distribution system in the Trauber media center (formerly the library) with a standalone video playback system in each classroom. The video distribution system provided the underlying infrastructure that allowed Trauber administrators to initiate plans for a daily in-house student-produced cable news program which eventually became *Trauber TV.*

A fundamental part of this third iteration technology plan allocated money to train teachers in the use of the newly installed computers and video system and to help them integrate student use of technology into their preexisting lesson plans. While there was considerable resistance on the part of Trauber's staff—many teachers felt that the technology was imposed on them by the district (and, of course, it was a mandate)—there were also technological evangelists who felt that this new equipment provided students with access to technology therefore helping to overcome the "digital divide."[2] The digital divide, shorthand terminology for the inequality of technology distribution that paralleled the inequities of income distribution throughout the United States, became crucial to understanding the motivations of technology leaders at Trauber.

Most teachers at Trauber eventually accepted the district's technological mandate to varying degrees, while continuing to be polarized around the twin concerns: the sense that technology was a "dangerous supplement" to their preexisting instructional methods and the fear that lower income students were victims of the digital divide. According to a district administrator overseeing technology during the height of Vista Valley's plan, most teachers readily accepted e-mail and online attendance procedures as part of their daily teaching routine, but resisted efforts to engage with technology during their actual instruction time. Of course, most teachers enjoyed using the newly installed computers for their own personal projects, but this use fell outside the pedagogical needs of their students. Realistically, the majority of teachers at Trauber, other than a core group of media and technology acolytes, failed to use the computers on a regular basis with their students and only programmed video as a reward for student behavior. The *Trauber TV* television program developed within the district's mandate for technology implementation, but had even more institutional leverage as it became a pet project of Vista Valley's superintendent of schools.

The Daily Practice of Media Education

My original assignment at Trauber was to teach Broadcast Communication Technology, a course originally designed as a grab bag of "below-the-line" technical skills training in camerawork, lighting, audio, and editing, peppered with "above-the-line" creative training in producing, writing, and directing. This course was funded in part by the vocational education district of which Vista Valley was a partner. In addition to broadcast technology, I taught an in-house video production course specifically for Trauber students that met no graduation or college admission requirements but was considered, instead, a recreational elective. What this meant in practice was that any student who caused trouble in more traditional academic electives was enrolled in my course because it was assumed to be a "fun" hands-on course that would not require students to do much beyond enjoy themselves. Nominal statements were made about preparing them for a career, but it was difficult to see how less than an hour of instruction a day was going to prepare educationally resistant students, without additional apprenticeship or college instruction, for even the world of public access cable television. At first, I tried to pretend that I was simply a vocational teacher by focusing on the basics of television production and seeking to please the former businessmen who ran the broadcast training program, but within a year, I decided to move my curriculum from a strictly vocational approach to one that favored a more critical outlook on media.

At the start of my second year at the school, district administrators made the decision to give students a daily, live news "broadcast" to be aired on the school's closed circuit television system. I worked with Trauber's principal and the district's director of educational technology to develop a television show that I felt met the informational needs of the school and the educational needs of my students.[3] I spent the fall training students in the skills necessary to produce a daily television program and the first *Trauber TV* cablecast aired in January 1995.[4]

The production process that I developed for the program involved students from all of my courses throughout the day: broadcasting, video production, and multimedia (which was part of an academy program that integrated professional skills with academic subject areas—English and American History). Students produced segments that focused on sports, activities, and programs at the school while also, on a much more limited basis with often much more limited results, producing short narrative features that allowed students to "express" themselves.[5] This mix of school sanctioned news, given a teenage spin, and expressive feature segments, alternating between adolescent angst and spoof, provided Trauber High with a mediated form of community that was otherwise lacking at a school of its size.[6] *Trauber TV* rapidly became the talk of the hallways, with mixed audience opinions ranging from irritation and mind-numbing boredom to amusement and rapt attention.

During the first class period of the day, students would rehearse the show. At the break between first and second periods, I would switch on the classroom television monitors and student animations and "challenging" music would pipe out through the school.[7] When the bell rang signaling the start of second period the show began, most often hosted by students from the school's drama or speech programs. *Trauber TV* opened many days with students performing parodic impressions of celebrities or popular television show hosts in place of traditional at-the-desk news anchors. This opening portion of the show, which included the mandatory flag salute,[8] was essentially a reading of the school's daily bulletin in some form of postmodern drag (and as with some of our celebrity parodies, literally in "drag"). In-studio guests and expanded information sessions with students and faculty members were followed by the day's featured student segment and a closing comment as we signed off. We then returned control of the classroom monitors to the teachers.

My approach to preparing students to work on the show originated from the lack of built-in articulation between my courses. In order to maintain a full day of video classes I enrolled all students who selected the course during whichever class period happened to fit with their schedules. This meant that, for the most part, I could not build upon skills that students received in beginning or intermediate classes, since all of my classes mixed student skill levels (this actually became an asset to my classes as the more advanced students assumed responsibility for more sophisticated productions and helped less experienced students to learn more advanced skills).

At the start of the school year I trained students for the first month on a core set of basic skills focusing on camera, audio, lighting, screen performance, and control room techniques (camera switching, audio mixing, and such), as well as on creating a team-based approach in a workshop-studio environment. I emphasized the community aspect of the course and the fact that, in place of a single teacher and fellow classmates as an audience for our work, we had the larger school community, and, potentially, district administrators as our audience. My approach to this aspect of the class parallels that suggested by Len Masterman:

> Dialogue ... involves a genuine sharing of power—even if differential power relationships exist outside of the dialogue.... It is genuinely a group process (rather than something which is engaged in by a number of discrete individuals) in which members recognize the power which can be generated through co-operative learning, group action and reflection, and are prepared to work through the group in order to maximize their own effectiveness.[9]

Students took this notion of audience seriously (as well as their new found power and influence) and set their standards high for the opening programs.[10] Following the first successful broadcast of the year, which usually occurred at the end of September, I always congratulated the students while reminding them, "Now the trick is to do it at the same level of quality one hundred and sixty more times." This, the daily pressure to produce, was the biggest obstacle to using a critical media education approach in a mixed academic-vocational setting. The repetitious nature of production, accompanied by the need to instruct students in new skills and concepts pertaining to more complex productions and the inherently distracted condition of being a teenager, led to the possibility for serious mistakes on a daily basis. I kept the show live, in contrast to live-on-tape, because it increased the performative aspect of the program and because it intensified the camaraderie and sense of responsibility amongst the student crew and performers.

Student-Produced Media as Indigenous Media

Media ethnographer Faye Ginsburg defines "indigenous media" as follows:

> [Indigenous media] respects the understandings of those aboriginal producers who identify themselves as members of "first nation" ... [a category] that index[es] the sense of common political struggle.
>
> [Media] evokes the huge institutional structures of television and film industries that tend to overwhelm local specificities and concerns for

relatively small populations while privileging commercial interests that demand large audiences as a measure of success.

[Indigenous media producers] exist in complex tension with the structures of dominant culture.[11]

This complex tension between small and big media written against the background of colonialism and globalization suggests comparisons with other forms of minority media production. Minority production is here defined as media aimed at a community of individuals with similar, yet distinctive, political-social-aesthetic interests and can be formed within indigenous, avant-garde, trash, ethnic, or youth populations. Each of these populations signifies an identity at odds with the dominant mode of media production.[12] Each in turn is transformed into a signifier by the dominant mode of media production. In this context, Ginsburg quotes Stuart Hall: "Identity is a production that is never complete, always in process, and always constituted within, not outside, representation."[13] As a subcultural formation, adolescence is an identity defined by the dominant social discourse while the identities manifested by teenagers are a response to this discourse (one does not simply choose to respond, one is compelled to respond). A particular identity is itself a representation—stolen, adopted, appropriated from a range of available representations at a moment of identity structuration.[14]

As has been shown in the case of *Blackboard Jungle,* teenagers have often been portrayed as primitives in need of acculturation. Education, embodied in the teacher as heroic figure, is seen as the force that can transform the immature student into the effective citizen. In media education, as a subfield of secondary education, production becomes twofold, relating at once to an explicit critique of the production of representations in a general sense and to the production of identity in the specific sense that Hall has in mind. Oedipal at root or not (recalling the earlier discussion of the beloved teacher as based on a model of psychoanalytic transference), the focus of much teen representation is organized around mocking or parodying the forms of adult performance as exemplified by the institutions of education and the media; at once a form of testing the self—trying on identities[15]—as much as it is a form of rebellion.[16]

As a matter of fact, there is a long history, and one that continues to this day in various forms of paternalism within global culture, that labels indigenous people using what anthropologist Harald E. L. Prins calls "the European primitivist stereotype of the 'noble savage' as child of nature."[17] By equating native people with children, colonial powers could freely dictate the terms in which sovereignty was enforced. According to colonialist logic, techniques of control were for "their"—indigenous peoples'—own good because Europeans possessed the rational thought and orderly conduct necessary for civilized governance while non-Western people possessed a simplicity in need of development. This notion of the noble savage, made famous in Montaigne's essay "On

Cannibals,"[18] alternated with the complementary concept of the "savage" as identified by Hobbes' notion concerning life before sovereign society as "nasty, brutish, and short."[19] Well-behaved (read compliant) indigenous populations were "noble" through innocence, yet when ill-behaved (read resistant) then the savages were most savage.

This oscillation between innocence and savagery has characterized much of the discourse regarding teenagers in American popular culture and public education. Teachers and educational administrators often reduce student expressive responses to the world as merely symptomatic of an immature or poorly formed worldview. This logic generates an educational practice that denies students agency for their actions and utterances by teaching them the proper "adult" way to express oneself in a range of social and cultural situations. For conservative educators, excessive or contrary forms of student expression must be repressed so as not to disrupt the content of learning, while, for liberal or progressive educators, student expression must be incorporated within the learning process, allowing a generalized notion of free expression to reign and consequently robbing individual student expression of efficacy or power. Both of these contradictory educational strategies create a subject population within a larger cultural binary of mature and immature, developed and undeveloped, mirroring the discourse that is often proffered regarding the thoughts and actions of non-Western groups and individuals.

Corollary to this twofold discourse of mature-immature is the relationship between agency and action. Agency as inscribed in action, imbued with the creativity of production and, indeed, revolution,[20] organizes my examination of the media work produced by students during my time at Trauber High. Consequently, this focus on agency and action inverts the metaphor of the child applied to indigenous people, replacing the excessive infantilization of teenagers with the positive expression of agency given to these same indigenous people in recent anthropological writing. This rationale of inversion that provides a metaphor of agency to be used as an analytical tool for examining student action, has a range of implications for pedagogy, but I want to focus on those that are specific to media education and in particular to my own teaching practice.

Consequently, the truism that teachers must trust students and be trusted in return guided my pedagogical practice while at Trauber. As a truism, it may seem trite, but it turns out to be exceptionally difficult to maintain in a public school setting. In the production-oriented and student-centered environment of media education, an opening must be provided, as much as the teacher has the power to do, for students to act autonomously (I was about to write semi-autonomously, which speaks to the fear of loss of control that grounds most pedagogical situations). Critical media practice depends on a measure of student autonomy as an a priori condition of deploying agency while using the media to communicate to a public (as an aggregate of peers and adult authorities). John

Dewey expresses well the problem that agency, he calls it "freedom" (a word that shimmers in its naughty clarity), presents for the teacher:

> It is not too much to say that an educational philosophy which professes to be based on the idea of freedom may become as dogmatic as ever was the traditional education which is reacted against. For any theory and set of practices is dogmatic which is not based upon critical examination of its own underlying principles. Let us say that the new education emphasizes the freedom of the learner. Very well. A problem is now set. What does freedom mean and what are the conditions under which it is capable of realization?[21]

It is easy to observe or experience classrooms that purport to be about the freedom of students, but in effect are about the personal charisma of the instructor and his or her disciples or are cages of chaos masquerading as experiments in progressive education. To provide students with agency, to relinquish as much personal or institutional power as a situation allows, is not to reject the need for responsibility. Bourdieu describes each setting, from the school to the state, as a field in which each individual holds a position in reference to others within that field. What one brings to this field are various forms of capital (cultural and economic) and the "sense of the game" one has gained from having lived within a set of determinants on one's actions—the family, school, media, etc.—one's habitus.[22]

Obviously, in one of the settings which Bourdieu cites as formative of cultural capital, the school, it is important to see the role of the teacher as at once embedded within the field of education while attending to the power effects (the relations of power and cultural capital) that play out within this particular field. Social actors, whether they are students, teachers, parents, or administrators, have variable accumulations of power, and the capital that is attained therein, as well as variable abilities (again, the sense of the game) for deploying accumulated power. There are teachers who, although set within the field of education as the authority, fail to use their structured role of power and are repeatedly overrun by their students until they either resign to coping or resign their position. While thinking within Bourdieu's framework one may decide that agency, "freedom" if you like, is determined by the field and the habitus, it is equally viable to think of the habitus and the field as texturing, giving the contours and surface to, freedom. The field determines the possible moves within the game while the habitus provides a feel for the game, and if this structuring of human agency can be seen as freedom at the level of subjectivity, then this is just the freedom that the teacher must convene for one's students.

Although Bourdieu's notion of the field has been faulted for being essentially a synchronic analysis of social power (the potentiality for a diachronic reading of habitus aside), by reading field and habitus against an educational perspective generated by imperatives for maturation of personality and development of emotional and cognitive faculties, a time-based analysis can be derived from Bourdieu's theoretical framework. In this possibly variant view, the field of secondary education coincides with the structural determinants indicated by the developmental time-field entitled "adolescence" while failing to provide rituals of maturation that would allow a truly developmental process to be realized. The arbitrary marker indicated by graduation from high school and the passing of one's eighteenth birthday breaks the enforced immaturity (that is enforced by the institutional restraints of law and education) while denying an adequate preparation for the responsibilities that are foisted upon the newly authorized adult. The field is not simply a spatial coordinate indicating one's "position" within the field, but also a temporal one, a time-field, which moves in relation to the temporal aspects of others within the field but also in relation to the changing structure, temporal and spatial, of the field itself.

However, one can imagine a field remaining structured for longer or shorter periods of time while other fields transform more rapidly in relation to one another. The relation of the changing structures would make the structures appear different to a position holder within a given field even if the field in which he or she were operating failed to change significantly. The algebra that describes these processes results from ratios, multiplications, and aggregations that are difficult to trace except as a glance from the corner of one's eye, but the results themselves, the larger structures that develop are easily visible given the right frame of reference.

Regis and Kathy Lee

The final year that I taught at Trauber, I was encouraged by having students enrolled in my senior level classes who brought sophisticated cultural and social references to *Trauber TV*, giving their productions a dash of wit and humor. The year began well; we started production at the end of September as we had the previous three years. I had trained this group of students in television production the prior year, as part of the junior level television production course, so they had the prerequisite technical skills and there was a good sense of cohesion and trust amongst the students. In addition, I had a strong personal connection with this group as a whole.

The first few shows followed a simple shooting structure using a single camera early in the week building to a more complex shooting style with multiple cameras by Friday. At the same time, student producers began developing what eventually became weeklong series focusing on a theme or idea meant to "spice" up the reading of the bulletin. *Trauber TV* students were aware of the difficulty of making the bulletin interesting, since essentially it consisted of club announcements, school notices, and the cafeteria menu, as this year's group had watched the previous three years worth of programs (*Trauber TV* had first aired their freshman year).

As the teacher responsible for overseeing the program, I had final approval for each series idea, but in an effort to democratize the process I required that student teams hold production meetings organized using dialogic group discussion methods suggested by Brazilian educational theorist Paolo Freire.[23] I saw my role as facilitating the development of each idea in light of my experience producing media while keeping an eye on issues that might unnecessarily provoke teachers, parents, and administrators (who provided the resources, financial and material, that allowed us to produce the show). Although by necessity my opinion carried the day, the process that developed with student producers opened up a space in which ideas and opinions could be freely expressed and a venue for discussing problems arising from technical, stylistic, and thematic concerns within individual episodes.

Some of our program ideas were quite successful with the school audience. Some were disasters that were abandoned by midweek. A few of the program ideas stirred controversy at the school (at times purposefully with an idea to generating debate, while at other times simply failing to judge audience response) and unfortunately led to attempts at censorship by a small, vocal group of teachers. Students repeated successful theme programs at occasional intervals throughout the year, each time improving technique and content to give the idea a fresh look. The unsuccessful "disaster" shows were critiqued—we watched each day's program with an eye to improving the next day's effort—and then the producing team responsible began work on ideas for new series.

By the third week of production, a team of student producers led by Troy and Phil, both members of the school's varsity football team, had developed a series of programs based on the network television morning talk show that at

FIGURE 4.1 "Regis" and "Kathy Lee" on *Trauber TV*.

that time was entitled *Live with Regis and Kathy Lee*. Their underlying premise was to parody the morning chat aspects of the show and to deliver the daily bulletin in this context. Neither of the students resembled either of the hosts, although Troy's mannerisms and vocal patterns evoked characteristics evident in Regis's style of delivery. Phil gave his Kathy Lee a more standardized treatment derived from comedic drag performances by such celebrities as Bob Hope, Milton Berle, and various *Saturday Night Live* regulars over the years.

"Regis," gestured with his coffee mug, commented on how great the coffee tasted, and made pleasant inquiries regarding "Kathy Lee's" son, Cody. Kathy Lee, beaming enthusiastically, provided viewers with a brief summary of Cody's recent activities. Both hosts would occasionally make reference to their beloved off screen floor manager Gelman (a typical trope from the actual program) who, played by a tall skinny girl serving as the floor director for that day's program, would poke her head into frame, smile and wave at the audience. The Gelman reference drew knowing laughs from the student crew during rehearsal and brought approving comments from other students throughout the day.

Many students and teachers seemed to be familiar with the show, even though it aired during the school day, and took delight in Troy's and Phil's particular take on the show and the manner in which they embedded the bulletin into their "morning chatter." In place of real sets, students developed virtual sets, which were keyed onto a green screen behind the performers. The video production program at Trauber had inherited discarded sets and props from the school's drama department and had collected odds and ends over the

FIGURE 4.2 "Regis" on *Trauber TV*.

years; some items abandoned by students, some items donated by parents. Out of these disparate materials, students, exhibiting the best in the *bricoleur* mentality, cobbled together a set for each day's show. For the Regis and Kathy Lee episodes, the student art director grabbed frames from a tape of the network morning show and digitally removed the "real" Regis and Kathy Lee, added in-studio chairs, a desk (painted with green chroma-key paint so as to provide a surface for the desk on the virtual set) and coffee mugs thereby providing a casual simulation of the original program. Although the size relationships changed throughout the show (the background remained the same size while the hosts' heads grew larger in close-up shots) the overall image communicated the desired effect—a *cinema povera* simulation of a sort.

Part of the appeal of these episodes was the campy, broadly humorous style of delivery by the hosts. Troy's boastful, tight shouldered Regis and Phil's mustached and goateed yet demure Kathy Lee mocked the conventions of the original, yet also showed admiration for the material being parodied through attention to detail and caricature. Due to their status as "jocks" Troy and Phil were also able to mock themselves in ways that students with less social status would not have been able to do without peer repercussions. To dress in drag— to "mess" with approved gender roles when one is still defining one's sexuality—and to act the buffoon are acts available only to those teenagers who have a strong sense of self-identity. Much is at stake with status among one's fellow students, but the show served to celebrate these differences as well as parody the ways in which network television represented them.

As a result of several episodes explicitly emphasizing difference as a positive marker of identity, *Trauber TV* became known amongst the student population

FIGURE 4.3 "Kathy Lee" on *Trauber TV*.

as a safe haven for "geeks," "stoners," "gangbangers," and "queer" students. I mention this as the school at large had many intolerant students and teachers who at times harassed students who identified with some of the above labels. So much of this type of harassment happened that eventually a former administrator and school board member helped initiate what became known as *Days of Respect*—several days each year when teachers and students discussed attitudes toward race, gender, and sexual orientation. Gay and lesbian issues were the most difficult to discuss and some teachers refused to participate due to religious or personal beliefs. Race, on the other hand, seemed to be the difference that everyone felt comfortable discussing. My own approach to the *Days of Respect* was to attempt to foster a respect for difference every day on *Trauber TV*. As it was, the gender-messing aspects of the *Live with Regis and Kathy Lee* segments became a fixture of our program and Troy and Phil returned several times over the year to host the show.[24]

Steel Cage Death Match

Teachers at Trauber responded in a more reactionary and more obvious way to a set of programs based on the Steel Cage Death Match episodes of the World Wrestling Federation's (WWF) television show. In the original show, celebrity wrestlers enter a steel cage and fight until one or the other of them is unconscious. High theater meets low sport. The announcers on these shows scream at and cajole the wrestlers as they fight, while egging on the audience into a frenzy. Much like the use of "morning chatter" to deliver the bulletin in the Regis and Kathy Lee format, the Steel Cage programs used the frenzy and excitement of professional wrestling—the hyperbole of the announcing and the simulated violence of the contestants—as another method for getting their fellow students to pay attention to the school bulletin.

The Steel Cage programs grew out of a single significant visual resemblance. One of my projects had been to build a cage out of chain link fencing materials in which to house the three studio television cameras as well as lighting and audio gear. Students thought that this storage space resembled the steel cage from the WWF matches and remarked on it at the opening of school. Knowing that the show had had problems in the past with simulated violence (many of the boys found violence amusing and gravitated toward producing feature segments that were simply spoofs of their favorite action adventure films), I emphasized that the student producers had to pay close attention to the tone of each of the Steel Cage segments. One of my main concerns was that students realize how a series featuring violence, whether obviously simulated or not, might feed into adult stereotypes (and paranoia) regarding dangerous, out of control teenagers as well as glorifying violent acts for their fellow students.

Many of the students in my courses were very familiar with the negative results of their actions (in the form of prohibitions through poor grades and referrals to the principal's office), but failed to link these negations to larger issues of power and the way in which one might work to negotiate with authority. Many of the *Trauber TV* students felt that they were "picked on" by adults at the school. And they were right in that most of their actions were understood and appreciated by their peers, but condemned by their teachers. What was seen by students as clever "riffs" on adult values and activities—harmless beyond the annoyance signaled by the adult involved—was seen by teachers as "disrespectful to authority" and therefore "unacceptable" during the school day. Since *Trauber TV* had an audience composed of both students and teachers, it seemed appropriate for me, as production supervisor, to serve both constituencies—students who found slapstick (physically violent humor) and parodies funny and teachers who felt threatened by this same kind of disruptive and authority-challenging humor. Weighing carefully the concerns of both groups of constituents, I decided to let the Steel Cage Death Match episodes proceed toward production. My overriding concern, in this instance, was to provide students with an interesting and humorous take on the consistently dry and dull school bulletin.

The first of the week's shows opened with a static shot of the steel cage storage area accompanied by hardcore thrash music playing on the soundtrack. The thrash rock songs definitely featured lyrics that were antiauthoritarian and libertarian in a vaguely reactionary way, but (following the standards set by the school administration) the lyrics featured no raunchy language or objectionable slang. I was dismayed at this choice of music, though the student director assured me that this was typical of WWF programs (replicating as closely as possible the authenticity of the original was very important to *Trauber TV* producers). Nevertheless I was uncertain how teachers would respond to the tone of the song lyrics and the harsh guitar sound. This was also a problem whenever we played hip-hop or rap on the show. Some teachers assumed that all rap music promoted the "gangsta" way of life so rap as a musical form should be banned as being inherently disrespectful to authority. In addition, *Trauber TV* had had problems before with "misreadings" by various staff members at the school. On one occasion students had produced a graphic that depicted the Warner Brothers' cartoon character the Tasmanian Devil seated in a cave surrounded by flames. Several of the evangelical Christians on staff were outraged that we were flaunting the "devil" on a school-produced program. I privately apologized to those that were offended for what seemed to be a miscommunication (in my eyes a gross misinterpretation), while stating emphatically that my students had done nothing wrong beyond appropriating a copyrighted image for creative purposes. In my role as supervisor of student-producers it was clear to me that there was an easily discernible, yet constantly shifting, demarcation between reasoned constraint on student ideas and outright censorship. This climate of implicit hostility to adolescent creativity serves as the background to the negative reception that the Steel Cage episodes received from faculty and staff.

FIGURE 4.4 Steel Cage Death Match on *Trauber TV.*

After the opening sequence of introductions, titles, and music, the school bulletin was performed as on other thematic shows throughout the *Trauber TV* year. While the hosts read the bulletin and taunted the contestants on the left side of the screen, on the right side various wrestlers entered the steel cage and fought "to the death." The onscreen fighting resembled wildly unrehearsed stage fighting and featured students who had portrayed "The Rock" and "Stone Cold" Steve Austin (WWF wrestlers famous at the time) in segments aired earlier in the year. The goofiness of the fighting and the overall lack of reality made the program register as a parody for students enrolled in my classes as well as for students throughout the school (as evidenced by classroom conversations, hallway eavesdropping, and e-mails from students).

As at other times throughout the year club members and school groups routinely came on the show to explain upcoming events and to promote their activities. During the week that the Steel Cage episodes aired, various guests appeared on the program. On the second day's episode, a club leader came on to plug the canned food drive that was happening that week, and, keeping in line with the WWF theme, he played the part of a wrestler who confronts the hosts, boasting about his skills while telling students to bring their cans to class and to collect them in the shopping bags provided for each teacher.

Protests to the school principal soon followed. Complaints centered on the notion that *Trauber TV* was promoting violence and that this was not a proper form for the reading of the daily bulletin. The principal and I had a discussion as to my intentions. It was always assumed that I had reasoned through my

FIGURE 4.5 Canned food drive on *Trauber TV.*

position in relation to each day's show (which in itself points to other assumptions on the part of the administration regarding my role in *Trauber TV* productions). The principal concurred that it seemed harmless enough, but requested, in an attempt to appease the offended teachers, that I place a disclaimer at the start of the show declaring that the violence was faked. We did add a disclaimer, but the complaints continued and we were asked to change the theme by midweek. Only three of the programs were aired.

The nature of this condemnation and the assumption of paternalism therein seem to derive from what media scholar Ellen Seiter refers to as a "lay theory" of media effects.[25] She suggests that those who see their role as protectors of children—a nurturing, yet controlling role—explicitly operate within a "trickle down" theory of how media influence children based on seemingly empirical studies conducted during the past thirty years. This type of study is quite familiar to news viewers who can easily discern the brief yet intense media panic that follows on the headlines that result from summarized findings. What Seiter calls lay theory also draws from the model of media inoculation used by those scholars and teachers who adhere to a critical pedagogy framework. Although proponents of critical pedagogy support giving agency to students, their rhetoric proceeds from the notion of "protecting" students against the devious methods of "mass media" as an initial step to empowerment. This form of critical pedagogy develops a binary of powerlessness through an emphasis on the overreaching power of the big media and the lack of power of the audience. The power to negate, to say "no" to the big media is denied as a de facto possibility for teens, and it remains to a select group of well-intentioned adults to provide a media decoding strategy for them.

In the case of the Steel Cage programs, many teachers felt threatened by the original WWF show—uninformed and uninterested in what desires *that* show puts into play—while feeling that by "reproducing" the WWF show, the students were simply vomiting up the worst that mass culture had to offer. What they failed to see, and what the student audience *did* most emphatically see, were the parodic changes made to the source material. At once, students were mocking the vital element of the WWF—macho dudes with loud, bellicose behavior—while celebrating a cultural artifact that they claimed as their own. Granted this was a boy cultural object, but at other times *Trauber TV* encouraged girl, queer, and geek cultural objects to be explored as well.

Augmentation: The Flows of Pedagogical Power

In their article on teaching video production to elementary school students, Donna J. Grace and Joseph Tobin state:

> Schools are highly stratified societies. They can be run like totalitarian states, banning satire, parody and protest, fearing the open discussion of difference, heterodoxy and inequality, and erecting emotional barriers between students and their teachers. Or they can be more like Bakhtin's vision of feudal societies, in which the rulers did not fear acknowledging their common humanity with the classes below them or creating spaces for dissent, satire and laughter.[26]

Leaving aside the correctness of their reading of Bakhtin, Grace and Tobin identify a crucial problem with opening the classroom to media production in a student-centered teaching environment. In their article, they mention elementary school students producing tapes that mock teachers, feature fart and vomit jokes, and depict the simulated torture and killing of animals. I am sure that the tone and content reflect the relatively harmless intent of elementary school students, but the subject matter and naughty behavior contained in these tapes call to mind much of the work produced by high school students at Trauber. Grace and Tobin indicate that the immediate response from teachers and administrators at their school was to try to censor student productions and to end the use of video production in the classroom altogether.[27] *Trauber TV* fared better by having the support of apparently more conscientious administrators (in particular the school principal and the district superintendent).

Grace and Tobin emphasize that for students the expectation of audience influenced the kind of tapes that were produced. Their students created videos that were meant to entertain and impress their peers and not the adults who administered the school. If students knew that adults would view their tapes, then the productions took on a more respectful, and often less inventive, approach toward their subject matter. Likewise, in response to the experience of having administrators cancel the Steel Cage episodes midweek, *Trauber TV* students became cognizant of the need to temper their more controversial ideas for audiences that included parents, teachers, and administrators (otherwise funding for the program may have been pulled).

While Grace and Tobin's support of "dissent, satire and laughter" is laudable, they fail to acknowledge the deeply entwined power relations that structure the social space of the school (the power relations with which the teacher-augmented mode negotiates). While it is easy to project a simple agonistic structure onto institutional power (in this case adult authorities suppressing the expression of students), a binary notion of power fails to account for the flows that circulate throughout the school, the parent community, and the political bodies (school boards and city councils) that determine to a great extent the particular shape of schooling. Parody and dissent are two ways in which students can interrogate this network of institutional power, while repression and critique are two ways that teachers and administrators, often bristling with contempt and fear, can respond.

The teacher-augmented mode, teachers and students sharing intellectual-symbiotic space with media (and *the media*), plays the wild card in this scenario in that it builds upon a cultural imaginary which can be read or interpreted through the legitimacy of popular culture snuck into the halls of academia (carried in on iPads, television, mobile phones, and, even, *Trauber TV* in the guise of professional media production). The complex power relations produced through, and by, the big media (which Ginsburg outlines in relation to indigenous production) are crucial to understanding the sociality of students and teachers when confronted with popular culture, but these same relations point toward the hierarchies that must be examined in any ongoing critique of corporate global media culture. The patterns (call them genres) and values (call them symbolic capital) that come into play while students are producing media are obviously set by the more grandiose, and indebted, forms of large scale media that most televisually literate student audiences confront on a daily basis.

Faced with the seemingly unstoppable influence of contemporary popular culture, teachers often transform their suspicion of the hold that media has on the intellectual and social life of students into displays of condescension and impatience with teenage culture as a whole, but this does not mean that power, and the responsibility for power, flows only one way from the teacher to student. As sociologist Barrie Thorne notes:

> Adults are said to socialize children, teachers socialize students, the more powerful socialize, and the less powerful get socialized. Power, indeed, is central to all these relationships, but children, students, the less powerful are by no means passive or without agency. As a parent and as an observer in schools, I have been impressed by the ways in which children

act, resist, rework, and create; they influence adults as well as being influenced by them.[28]

Thorne's observation becomes even more salient if it is understood in the context of Foucault's well-known reformulation of power as residing "everywhere; not because it embraces everything, but because it comes from everywhere."[29] As Foucault's reformulation suggests, while there are obvious quantitative effects of power (the larger the resources, the more repression and coercion can be applied in a given situation), the notion of having and deploying power in the Steel Cage incident further problematizes the duality inherent in the ways that critical media pedagogy has theorized power. In the narrative that coalesced around the Steel Cage episodes, vehemently promulgated by some teachers at the school, students acted inappropriately because I had not supervised, read disciplined, them sufficiently. While slapstick may be appropriate in settings outside the school, perhaps on cable television in the evenings or at the movies on the weekends, the same popular forms of humor are off limits in the structurally stabilized environment of the classroom. In this scenario, students acted as pawns in a relationship governed by expanding circles of power that began with my role as teacher in the classroom, then moved outward to include the supervisory role of administrators at the school and the district, and finally ending with much of the blame being placed on the role of the cable and network programmers at the national level (at the time WWF programs and their spin-offs had exploded filling a lot of screen time throughout the week). This tiered system of power relations—students, classroom teachers, school and district administrators, and cable television executives—represents the circles of a Dante-like media hell stealing agency from those on the bottom while distorting through a folk form of technological determinism the actual resources available to those powerful entities at the top.

The students' choice of the WWF as vehicle for enhancing the school bulletin, my blunder in failing to see how simulated violence played upon the fears of my fellow teachers, and the teachers' anger at the seeming immorality of the Steel Cage programs, all represent spatial locations (at minimum drawing upon the mental, social, and biological interests of the participants) that existed, at that time, within the field of power relations at Trauber High—drawing on Bourdieu's formulation of the exercise of power as "position-takings" by agents with competing interests who bring differing histories and qualities of self to a given field.[30] This notion of position-takings is key to understanding the teacher augmented. Power relations that appear as static within a field, positions frozen in place over time, such as is usually understood as pertaining to the authoritarian hierarchies dominant in school settings, are constantly at odds, and proven to be illusory, when confronted with the shifting set of positions taken, exchanged, refused, and subverted by teens as they move toward adult consecration. In the field that delimits education, the authority conferred upon the teacher by the classroom, the cheek of the students in the hallways, and the storm of persuasive and mesmerizing power effects generated by the media represent several of the power fields that come into contact during media-based pedagogy. The need for stability in the classroom, what is called classroom management in educational jargon, constantly undergoes challenge as the field of adolescence becomes increasingly identified with the more determining power relations emanating from entertainment and the media culture at large.

In this context, the teacher-augmented mode of pedagogical agency necessarily transforms the power relations, for better or for worse, between all of the players in the field of education. As has been evident throughout this chapter, there are no clear-cut guidelines, or even maxims, that could claim to guide the production of pedagogy in the teacher-augmented mode (as there were for the teacher-presented mode and as evidenced by Capretz's control of his program and its use in the classroom). The wilding that is inherent in the most integral forms of the teacher augmented, and the subversion to authority that necessarily follows, finds a containing force in the move from augmentation to embodiment. The teacher embodied, which will be discussed at length in the chapter that follows, opens out onto an even less explored terrain, one that may presage more repressive (or more hopefully, liberating) forms of pedagogy in the future.

5

STEVE

The Teacher Embodied

Clearly the machine is not going to replace the teacher—indeed, it may create a demand for more and better teachers if the more onerous part of teaching can be relegated to automatic devices. Nor does it seem likely that machines will have the effect of dehumanizing learning any more than books dehumanize learning. A program for a teaching machine is as personal as a book: it can be laced with humor or be grimly dull, can either be a playful activity or be tediously like a close-order drill.

—Jerome Bruner, *The Process of Education*[1]

In Orson Scott Card's science fiction novel, *Ender's Game,*[2] Earth's military command selects ten-year-old Ender Wiggin to attend Battle School and, upon promotion, Command School. At these institutions of military training, students learn to engage in combat by playing an immersive ("serious") game that simulates intergalactic warfare. Over the several years that follow, Ender masters gameplay and excels at leading spaceships full of children-warrior-players in tactical maneuvers against the "buggers," an insectlike alien species at war with Earth.

At the novel's conclusion, following a series of exhausting battles in which he sacrifices the lives of many of his fellow players, Ender finally engages in an all-out assault on the bugger home world. In the final attack, having learned to play like no other before him, he displays a reckless, tenacious brutality verging on barbarity. He readily deploys the weapon known as the "little doctor," a device that destroys the bugger queen and, through her, the entire bugger civilization.

As the bugger home world explodes, Mazer, a legendary commander from the first bugger war, steps forward from the bloc of military brass that has been observing Ender's play. He explains that the simulation on which Ender trained for years had, in fact, been seamlessly replaced with a media-interactive command structure that allowed for actual battle to take place based on Ender's gameplay. Earth's commanders needed Ender to believe that his moves were merely actions in a game so that he would exploit his knowledge of bugger psychology fully while taking necessarily extreme actions to overcome his foe.

Card's novel pivots on the morality involved in supplanting virtual with actual combat. By using a game simulation, Earth's military sought to dampen Ender's emotional affect, the compassion that serves as a brake on operational forms of violence and savagery, while masking the destructive actuality of effective warfare. This deception highlights what Card's narrative suggests drives military simulation and military-based interactive games: an ethos of *performative realism*. An attempt to create interactive transparency (an illusion that stands in for what we perceive to be the casual verisimilitude of everyday life) is what organizes the production agenda of the entertainment industry, the military, and the computer research centers that design and implement the code at the heart of the video games, special-effects blockbusters, and interactive simulations that these institutions produce and distribute. Performative realism provides the conceptual ground out of which the teacher-embodied mode of pedagogical agency develops.

Performative Realism: Saddam Hussein, Buggers, and Klingons

According to Richard Lindheim, founding Executive Director of the Institute for Creative Technologies (ICT) at the University of Southern California (USC) in Los Angeles (and a former television producer who oversaw the *Star Trek* franchise for Paramount), the Pentagon originally approached him to create a military simulation system saying, "We've been thinking of what the ICT should do. Very simple, why don't you develop the holodeck from *Star Trek*."[3] As *Star Trek* fans know, the holodeck was a simulation room featured in the *Star Trek: The Next Generation* television series. While in the holodeck, crewmembers could touch objects generated by a holographic virtual reality system and even appear to travel back in time (a concept that was featured in several episodes of *The Next Generation* series). Through the evocation of a holodeck-style simulation system, the ICT's military sponsors were merely using an easily accessible idea from popular culture to serve as a metaphor for directing their research agenda. That the ICT was founded as a confluence of entertainment media, military training, and computer science helps to explain how science fiction can become a model for research, especially since *Star Trek* centers on thrilling tales of a federation space ship exploring and at times policing the boundaries of the universe. As the ICT is part of an initiative at USC, known for its close ties to Hollywood, and funded by the U.S. Army it seems easy to extrapolate that the holodeck would suffice as a romanticized vision of what a collaboration between the military and the entertainment industry could hope to achieve.

While seeking to explain to a lay audience the multiple applications that could result from research at the ICT, Lindheim remarked: "The same engine can be used for education or entertainment, or for a networked game. What's the difference between fighting Saddam Hussein and fighting Klingons? It's just different applications of the same technology."[4] Of course, Saddam Hussein, even after his execution by the reconstituted Iraqi state, existed as an actual person living in the world, while the Klingons are a fictional, and, given the status of the *Star Trek* series, one could say mythical, race of beings often at war with humans. Lindheim demonstrates a troubling ethical slippage between the ongoing, lived worlds of daily life, whether in a combat zone or in New York City, and the fictional worlds being developed by the ICT.

Lindheim's remarks linking education and entertainment, Saddam Hussein and Klingons, suggest the assumed ease with which the military objectives of simulation training are predicated on a naïve form of realism, such that simulated battle and actual combat are interchangeable (in ways that also easily evoke *Ender's Game*).[5] The premise of the ICT training simulations is to prepare officers for military command in hostile combat situations. One army spokesperson explained during an interview with CBS News: "The most dangerous time for a soldier is the first two weeks of combat." This goal, to get past the early learning phase of battle (in which if one fails, one may die), implies that the simulations are capable of miming reality and thus providing the experiential lessons necessary to save a soldier's life. Or, as a brigadier general demonstrating the ICT virtual reality headgear for the same CBS *Sunday Morning* program observed: "It feels very real…. This is the kind of simulation that makes you sweat." In other words, the acuity of the visual and aural interface generated physical responses in the brigadier general that allowed him to experience the simulation at an emotional and corporeal level.

Therefore, for the ICT researchers there needed to be more than simply a visual and auditory correspondence between the rendering of the virtual human scenario and the world of actual combat, there also needed to be a representational realism that affected the body directly. Users must perform as if the representations and narratives of the simulation had consequences for the body at the level of movement, emotion, and situational understanding. In this regard, the rendering of the virtual humans in a visual style drawn from, and consciously evoking, video games linked the interaction and training of the military's new media with that of the performance of gameplay. The sweat of conflict and speed of action during a first-person shooter game are exactly what the ICT researchers hoped to achieve in their training scenarios.

As media theorist Nicholas Garnham has suggested, "Any serious student of the media, their future impact and development needs, therefore, to take seriously the cost-benefit, means-ends thinking of engineers. Indeed the specific visions of technological use and development that such engineering thinking may at any time favor and propagate can only be critiqued if it is first understood."[6] As for the engineers, so for the military and their motives of efficiency and economy that drive much of the research design and implementation at the ICT. And, as new media writer Allucquére Rosanne Stone suggests, "It is impossible to study the emergence of virtual systems without acknowledging the overwhelming influence exerted upon the entire field of virtual technologies research by the military."[7] So this chapter has a twofold purpose, to examine the assumptions and intentions of the ICT researchers and their military sponsors and to determine to what extent these assumptions and intentions become mapped onto the agent systems that are developed at the institute.

While previous chapters focused on the teacher as a figure presented by the screen, either as a character within the narrative or as a teacher enacting pedagogy through the screen to a student audience, or as a teacher augmented by the technology of the media in relation to his or her class of students, this chapter explores the interactions that result when the flesh-and-blood teacher is replaced by a nonhuman teaching agent that retains the interactive aspects of the augmented mode of instruction. This final transformation of instructional practice results in the teacher as figure and function being embodied by the pedagogical agent within a simulated environment delivered through a screen interface.

STEVE, a Pedagogical Agent

In the late 1990s, computer science researchers working at the Center for Advanced Research in Technology for Education (CARTE) at the Information Sciences Institute (ISI)—the research unit at USC that spun off the Institute for Creative Technologies—developed an intelligent agent system that they christened STEVE.[8] This agent was designed to provide Navy personnel with training in the operation of submarines. In the training simulation, Steve appears onscreen as a cartoon figure, a male head and torso without legs, which floats around a detailed rendering of a specific class of Navy sub.

The simulated interior of the submarine, along with Steve as a training partner, appear onscreen from the perspective of the human user—similar visually to the way in which a player experiences a "first person shooter" video game. If additional navy cadets train at the same time, all of the human users appear to each other as avatars that resemble a disembodied man's hand and head, with jet black hair, hovering and moving along with Steve through the steel encased rooms of the submarine. Steve's lack of legs, and the strange appearance of the other avatars, was explained by Jim Avery, a lead researcher at ISI, as resulting from the extensive computer processing power needed to drive the interactive teaching and figure animation embedded within the Steve agent system. To supply Steve with legs would have limited the amount of processing that could be dedicated to the problem solving and language recognition features that

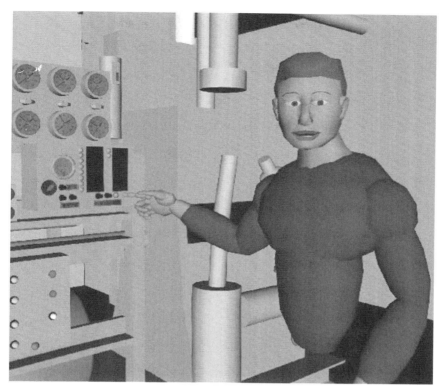

FIGURE 5.1 STEVE demonstrates the functions of a submarine. (USC Institute for Creative Technologies, 1999)

drive Steve's instructional interactions with the user. Legs become superfluous at this point in the design of the simulation, as does a realistic rendering of the Steve agent, because a sense of realism in the scenario is secondary to the actual goal of training recruits to function in the modeled operational environment of a submarine.

As a trainee moves through the sub, objects and control panels appear while an onscreen textual interface inquires as to the actions that should be taken at that particular juncture. The actions called for are simple and procedural in nature. Questions appear onscreen in a window: "Which button should be pressed?" or, "How often should the oil be checked?" All of the questions regarding these mechanical procedures are laid out in the order necessary to operate the submarine effectively. As each of the tasks is being completed, Steve hovers nearby providing cues as to the sequence of actions that must take place. If the user fails to follow the sequence correctly (or waits too long to respond), Steve glides into frame and provides teaching machine style instruction on the appropriate procedures.

An example: Steve floats to the area of the sub in need of attention and in a mechanical-synthesized voice says, "That goal is relevant because it will allow us to check the alarm lights." Onscreen he points to the alarm light button. If the user fails to press the alarm light button, Steve repeats his previous instruction using the same repetitive robotic tone, "I suggest that you press the function test button." Regardless of the peril to the sub presented by the situation, Steve carries out his interactions with the human-user in a flat unmodulated tone of voice (which calls to mind HAL 9000, from the film *2001: A Space Odyssey*, and evokes a petit, and amusing, nightmare of the affectless teaching machines discussed in chapter 2). As Jeff Rickel and his colleagues (programmers and designers of the Steve agent system) note:

> Steve has no emotions. While this makes him a patient and tolerant collaborator, it leads to … serious limitations…. Because his teaching is emotionally flat, it is not motivational, and Steve is unable to distinguish mundane instructions (e.g., "To check the oil level, pull out the dipstick") from important ones (e.g., "Whatever you do, don't push that red button!").[9]

This lack of emotional affect is, of course, contradictory to the pedagogical approach that made *French in Action* so popular—Pierre Capretz's playful sense of humor as teacher and as scriptwriter. In his telecourse, Capretz invested his onscreen personality with a prankster's take on storytelling and pedagogy while relying heavily on French New Wave cinema for the program's visual and narrative style. These qualities of personality, play, and passion are exactly what Steve lacks.

On the other hand, Steve does provide a structured tutorial in which the main functions of the submarine are laid out in an easily learnable and linear fashion. While the experience differs considerably from actually visiting a submarine, the Steve simulation does familiarize recruits with a schematic and operational knowledge of a Navy sub. This experiential approach to learning organizes the content of the Steve simulation as a whole. But the individual instructions that Steve gives to a user do not constitute the totality of the instructional content. Rickel and his fellow programmers state:

> [In simulations] students can learn about ancient Greece by walking its streets, visiting its buildings, and interacting with its people. Scientists can envision life in a colony on Mars long before the required infrastructure is in place. The range of worlds that people can explore and experience is unlimited, ranging from factual to fantasy, set in the past, present, or future.[10]

And this is exactly the approach that they use in the Steve scenario: a user learns about the design and operation of a submarine by walking its corridors, visiting its rooms, and "interacting with its people" (Steve and the other user-avatars present in the simulation).

This early version of the Steve pedagogical agent shows limitations on several levels, in addition to the concerns enumerated by the computer scientists who designed him. First, his cartoon appearance reifies his pedagogical interactions for the user-learner. While an actual submarine has solidity and a spatial relationship to the body of a Navy recruit, the Steve scenario appears within a representational framework most often associated with cartoon characters such as Daffy Duck and the Road Runner. While this cartoon "reality" has been justified by researchers at the ISI in reference to another of their agent training systems that counsels mothers on how to interact with their children sick with cancer (the irreality of the simulation lessens the fear and gravity of the situation), the visual rendering of the Steve agent provides little in the way of realizing the physical and affective qualities that should go into a successful embodiment of a pedagogical agent along the lines that have been addressed so far.

Second, Steve's manner of addressing human users erases the specificities of human interaction. The two concepts that ISI researchers mentioned as being key to Steve's instructional persona are "politeness" and "the media equation."[11] Reduced to its simplest formulation by CARTE researcher Lewis Johnson, the empirical studies of communication researchers Byron Reeves and Clifford Nass find that:

> People rate computer programs that praise and flatter them more highly than they rate programs that do not. People ascribe personalities to programs, and prefer programs whose apparent personality traits are similar to their own. People respond to politeness (and rudeness) in programs just as they do to politeness and rudeness in people. Embodied interfaces exploit the "Media Equation" by reinforcing people's natural tendency to interact with computers as they do with people.[12]

On this point, another prominent researcher at the ICT remarked that every action an agent performs, intentional or not, is read by users as having emotional content. Given this proposition, then, the peculiar affectless qualities of expression generated by the Steve agent as he interacts onscreen will be "ascribed" by the user as a signifier of the agent's personality, one that is at odds with most conventional notions of appealing human emotion. This misalignment of intention on the part of the agent, much of it a consequence of Steve's computer architecture within the limitations of computing power, creates an interference to the affective qualities which signify "human" and consequently garbles the effectiveness of Steve's pedagogy.

To many of those users who have encountered this early version of Steve, his most salient feature was his unintentional humor. Steve's flatly comical reminders to "push the alarm button" recall the images of the stereotypically "bad" teachers who drone on in numerous Hollywood campus comedies (and often actually people the hallways of America's elementary and secondary schools). Steve's designers were obviously aware of this peculiar facet of his personality, as well as his more overt pedagogical deficiencies, and emphasized in response, during our interviews, that all ISI and ICT projects are "advanced research." Therefore Steve and the other pedagogical agents at the institutes are meant to pave the way for more functional and deployable products at a later time.

One example of a more realized, and commercially viable, product that resulted from advanced research at the ICT was the *Full Spectrum Warrior* video game. *Full Spectrum Warrior* began as an attempt by ICT researchers to use an "off the shelf" game engine (the programming software that drives gameplay and character/scene rendering) to design a military training videogame for the U.S. Army. Having completed a game that met the specifications demanded by the Army, the ICT researchers built upon this underlying programming a different and more generic commercially viable videogame that allowed a consumer to command a platoon of soldiers in what appears to be Iraq. The original version of *Full Spectrum Warrior* won numerous awards and, according to the information provided by the ICT, had become one of the best-selling video games as of 2005. While this game differed from the Steve scenario in that it did not include any intelligent agents—the platoon under one's command responds to the orders using a more simplified artificial intelligence architecture—it did point toward applications of the agent systems in ways that could more fully exploit the performative realism that served as the goal of the ICT simulations.

MRE and SASO-ST @ ICT

Steve moved from CARTE to the Institute for Creative Technologies where the project saw further development through funding provided by the U.S. Army. One of several later iterations based on the Steve agent code, the Mission Rehearsal Exercise (MRE), featured three independent pedagogical agents within its virtual environment. In the scenario that serves as the narrative arc for this simulation, each agent provides varying levels of instructional functionality. The agent with the highest level of interactivity is "The Sergeant" who directly addresses the user as "Sir" and "Lieutenant." The Sergeant requests decisions from the user regarding conflicts that arise within the narrative, suggests possible solutions, and leads the troops under his command. Two less functional agents, a mother figure and Tucci the medic, are capable of interacting with the user (the mother accuses the Lieutenant-user of failing to help her son), but most often they simply interact with the Sergeant as he relays the input from the user to those involved within the simulation. Unlike Steve, the virtual humans of the MRE (the Sergeant, the Mother, and Tucci) all have complete bodies rendered in a semi-photo-realistic style comparable to images present in successful consumer videogames at the time.

During my research on pedagogical agent and virtual human projects at the ICT, I was invited to attend two troubleshooting sessions that focused on problems with character rendering, speech recognition, and overall programming issues for the MRE simulation and another iteration of Steve that had been rewritten from the bottom up entitled SASO-ST. The two sections that follow are constructed using observational data from these troubleshooting sessions and are intended to provide the reader with a glimpse into the experience of the user interface and immersive environment for which each scenario was designed.

MRE: April 4, 2004

Stepping into the widescreen projection room at the ICT calls to mind the experience upon entering an IMAX movie theater at a local theme park. Although the scale of the experience is considerably reduced at the ICT, the immersive quality of the IMAX experience dominates. The audience at the ICT's Virtual Reality (VR) demonstration room is presented with a large wrap-around screen and the latest in audio and image projection technologies. While the ICT's screen might be dedicated to presenting cutting-edge research that combines artificial intelligence (AI) and real time animation technologies, nevertheless the whiff of IMAX's origins in a cinema of attractions from the silent movie era and the boardwalk rollercoaster lingers throughout each ICT demonstration.[13] And perhaps this is as it should be since the ICT's goals are to use the best techniques for immersive reality drawn from the entertainment industry and apply these same techniques to the training needs of the military, making it a cinema of attractions geared to combat during wartime.

Scattered throughout the small theater, personnel from the Institute for Creative Technologies, the USC Viterbi School of Engineering, and Jim Avery (one of Steve's original designers) from CARTE sit waiting for the test to begin. A technician seated behind a workstation with a stack of computers fiddles with digital gear at the back of the room.

Larry Rasmussen, a key cognitive science researcher at the ICT, turns to the technician: "Run test version."

Someone in the darkened room says: "We might want to consider this version as our demo version."

Someone else interrupts: "Some things may need to be taken out...."

The simulation begins with a live action film sequence—once again relying on the dominant perspectival viewpoint made conventional by first-person shooter videogames—in which the user (addressed as the Lieutenant) rides in a military vehicle and happens upon a traffic accident in a small Bosnian town. As the Lieutenant climbs out of the transport, an African American Sergeant approaches to explain what has happened. Apparently another vehicle in the Lieutenant's squadron has struck a young boy while attempting to avoid a collision with a civilian vehicle. The boy's mother cries in agony as her son lies on

FIGURE 5.2 The mission rehearsal exercise scenario in the ICT screening room. (USC Institute for Creative Technologies, 2004)

the ground possibly fatally injured. A medic kneels over the boy and assesses his condition. As the opening scene dissolves into the animated image from the MRE simulation, the live actors are replaced by intelligent agent counterparts and the Sergeant-agent awaits a response from the Lieutenant-user. During an interview, the MRE project manager explained that a Hollywood screenwriter had been commissioned to write the MRE scenario—the opening sequence and the simulation that follows. It was hoped by the design and programming team that the entertainment industry professional would provide the MRE narrative with greater dramatic conflict thereby giving the user more emotionally charged decisions to make.

The simulation's immersive image spreads across three overlapping computer projections that are precisely registered making the large wraparound picture appear seamless. A few minutes into the test the left screen switches from a portion of the overall image to a graphical user interface with a series of overlapping windows each of which streams computer code from top to bottom. The simulation scenario continues to play across the center and right screens.

Someone comments: "Can we do something about the mother's face." Laughter titters throughout the room. The problem is obvious to all. The mother's face is dark brown while her neck and hands are almost white. At intervals her face shoots out from her head as if it were rapidly expanding and contracting.

The Sergeant-agent approaches. A slightly bemused smile on his face, he stares out at the audience. In the background the mother pulls at her clothes and cries while Tucci the medic administers aid to her wounded boy. Several Army vehicles are parked in the distance and troops mill about while awaiting further commands.

Rasmussen, talking into an audio headset, addresses the Sergeant-agent onscreen: "Who is hurt?" The agent sways a bit—apparently on the balls of his feet—and grins, but doesn't respond to Rasmussen's question.

Rasmussen awaiting a response from the agent grows frustrated: "Stop smiling at me." A rattle of noise from the back of the room suggests a flurry of troubleshooting as the technician attempts to fix the voice recognition problem. He signals to Rasmussen to try speaking to the agent again.

Rasmussen, to the Agent on screen: "What should we do now?"

The Sergeant-agent doesn't realize that Rasmussen is talking to him, but says, "Secure the area," to his troops as they continue to wander through the background performing vaguely militarylike actions—pointing their rifles and searching the bushes.

The Sergeant-agent turns and shouts for the squads to move. It seems like quite a long delay between the agent's command and the response by his squads. As if on some invisible cue (it must be a lag in the computer processing necessary to understand the Sergeant's command), they move into position.

Several explosions appear onscreen accompanied by silence on the soundtrack. The three primary agents flinch at the blasts (lacking sound), but the auxiliary characters in the background do not respond as they carry on with their repetitive movements.

Someone notes: "Pretty lame explosions, but everyone ducked I noticed."

Rasmussen: "Sergeant, send two squads forward."

The Sergeant-agent finally responds to Rasmussen: "Sir, that is a bad idea. We shouldn't divide our...."

Loud Explosion! Although he fails to flinch this time, there appears a slightly bewildered look on the agent's face.[14]

Someone comments: "His reaction is a little slow."

Onscreen, the mother seems to be in increasing agony, as she attends to her injured son. Her actions call to mind, unfortunately, the stereotypical model of the hysterical female.

Someone laughs and says: "Soldiers are going through the trucks."

The squads as they move into position seem to be walking through the trucks and the sides of buildings. As the whole scenario increasingly begins to resemble a comical animated film, the extraneous troop movements take on the look and feel of zombies from typical B horror movies. It becomes clear that all of the pedagogical agents are in effect blind. They are programmed to pretend that they are sighted—looking in the general direction of the Lieutenant-user and smiling—but they respond to the world outside of the simulation based solely on the vocal interactions that are initiated by the user.

An angry mob of local people emerges from behind one of the buildings near the horizon. They move about as a group in the distance as they gesture defiantly at the troops. Green smoke drifts up from the center of the mob. A helicopter flies into frame and hovers overhead. On the audio track someone barks an unintelligible command over a walkie-talkie, but the helicopter makes no noise.

The Sergeant-agent speaks to Rasmussen: "Area secure, sir. L2 is secure, sir."

Rasmussen surveys the chaos arising onscreen from the angry mob and the hysterical mother, then comments to no one in particular: "He is such a liar."

While all of this happens, machine code—binary data in the form of strings of numbers—spills wildly down the left hand screen. "Medic 108258081... Agent" appears in a window on the code screen. Throughout the room people are commenting on the code as it flows past. While I have been concentrating on the two screens that contain the visual representation of the simulation, others in the room, presumably programmers, have been focusing on reading, perhaps debugging would be the more appropriate word, the code as it appears.

Again, a small string of the code passes by: Mom 102... Agent.

Someone says, "Stuck in output speech."

On the other two screens, Tucci the medic talks to the Lieutenant-user, but no audio plays.

Someone says: "I didn't hear much of the medic's voice."

Rasmussen: "There seem to be a number of audio issues."

The helicopter continues to hover in space above the squads as they move toward the angry mob and its plume of green smoke. This bit of narrative seems to be stuck at the point where the troops are moving into position to engage the mob. The helicopter hovers, the troops move forward a little, but the narrative fails to progress.

Rasmussen: "We need to totally rethink the audio architecture."

Avery: "When we do a demo, we should be able to hear the medic's voice."

Someone else comments: "Do we have to ask questions of the medic?"

Suddenly, a percussive audio blast of whirring helicopter blades erupts from the speakers, startling everyone, then cuts out. Some chuckle at what has become the finale of the test. Others rub their ears hoping for relief. Rasmussen and his team leave to work on resolving some of the problems discovered during the session.

SASO-ST: December 8, 2004

Splayed across the screen are a series of overlapping operating system windows. Lines of computer code rain down the main system window calling to mind the now iconic images from the film *The Matrix*. In another window appears a list of file folders containing key elements of another of the ICT's training scenarios, SASO-ST (short for "Stability and Support Operations Simulation and Training"). I have been invited to this test by the ICT project manager in an attempt to correct my perception that the MRE simulation seemed to be full of bugs. I was assured that SASO was a more stable project from a design and programming perspective.

The three rows of seats are filled mostly with personnel from the ICT. A technician sits at a workstation with a stack of computers and other digital gear at the back of the room. The room overflows with people. There are not enough chairs for everyone.

The scene on the screen is a dimly lit triage room. The patients who inhabit the triage area are visually coded as foreign (dark skin, black hair, Arabic dress), while the female doctor, who is attempting to calm a woman clad from head to toe in black, has blond hair and wears a starched, white hospital smock. A fly buzzes about the room, appearing at times to be extremely large as it closes in on the viewer's perspective. In the background there is a whiteboard covered with marks scribbled in red and black marker. Blood has splattered across the wall and there are pools of blood on the cracked and worn wooden floor. The wallpaper is torn and degraded.

Hospital cots fill the room. Several of the cots are dressed with sheets soaked red with blood. On one cot lies a man with a severed arm and leg. He waves his stumps in the air. Coagulated blood smears the white gauze that covers each of his severed limbs.

FIGURE 5.3 The triage room from the SASO–ST scenario. (USC Institute for Creative Technologies, 2005)

On the couch in the right hand corner of the room, a small girl weeps while rocking back and forth on her knees. As the scene progresses, it becomes apparent that each of these digital characters repeats their individual movements on what appears to be a loop. The man with severed limbs rotates his bloody stumps again and again, the nurse reassures the black clad woman with the same gesture over and over, and the girl on the couch wails and rocks.

From within the darkened theater someone asks when the test is going to begin. Someone else answers, "We're waiting for the doctor." A man in the back of the room turns to the technician and says, "You can go ahead and run it." The angle on the room changes abruptly as the point of view of the camera (again following closely the conventions of first-person shooter video games) appears to sweep across the scene and then move through a door. A male doctor with tanned skin and curly black hair beneath a surgeon's cap appears in frame. He leans against the edge of a wooden desk, holding a cup of coffee in his right hand, staring intently out at the audience.

Arabic writing can be seen on the tapestry that covers a side wall of his office. The back wall has a large observation window through which the patients on the cots in the triage room are seen. Along the bottom edge of the window frame are packing boxes and crates. Tacked to one wall are charts diagramming troop movements.

On the left side screen folders that read "verbal communication," "Doctor's environs," and "emotions in the global context" sit nested within a window floating above a sea of programming code. At the top corner of this screen is another window filled with a series of sliders charting the status of the Doctor's emotions. These sliders read simply: "joy," "hope," "distrust," "fear," "anger," "guilt," and "anxiety."

"Hello," the Doctor loudly proclaims. His speaks with a strong accent as he firmly crosses his arms across his chest. From somewhere in the darkened VR theater an audience member comments, "Scary man." Someone else adds that the Doctor is taking his "avoidance stance." Another asks, "How is his trust changing?" As the Doctor changes position, the sliders representing his level of emotional composure appear to fluctuate.

The Doctor addresses the man in the back of the room who initiated the simulation, "Sir, we're trying to help this patient." The Doctor's accent is difficult to place. Is it Arabic, Spanish, or the result of audio distortion? There is an echo or reverberation each time the Doctor speaks. The Doctor addresses the man in back—the "user"—as "Captain." In the SASO-ST scenario, the conflict arises when an Army Captain (the user) must convince the Doctor to move his makeshift hospital to a safer location. What the Doctor does not know, but intuits from the remarks of the Captain, is that the site upon which the hospital is located is scheduled to be shelled by artillery in the next few days. The Doctor plans to bargain with the Captain-user to try to acquire transportation vehicles and medical supplies for his hospital in exchange for agreeing to

FIGURE 5.4 Doctor Perez from the SASO-ST scenario. (USC Institute for Creative Technologies, 2005)

move his facility. The officer-training component arises from the user's need to negotiate the best deal for the U.S. Army while convincing the Doctor to agree to move his hospital.

The Doctor speaks again, "We can reach an agreement." This time what he says is distorted, but the words are recognizable. Then he spurts out a series of repeated words that are distorted and garbled beyond recognition.

Compared to Steve and MRE, SASO-ST has a very detailed look to it. The walls, furniture, and clothing are deeply textured and cast shadows that give a sense of realism to the location and its characters. On the audio track, bomb and fan sounds shake the floor of the VR theatre (we have been told that special subwoofer speakers have been installed so that the audience can feel the impact of the bombs as they explode).

The onscreen Doctor smiles and says: "Very nice to meet you." Looking at the emotion sliders on the left hand screen, it is obvious that someone has increased the agent's familiarity quotient. The Doctor continues: "What do you want?"

Larry Rasmussen, again leading the test, says to the Doctor, "It's not safe here." Doctor: "Say again." Without prompting on the part of Rasmussen, the Doctor continues, "Look at these people. Do you see that girl? She lost her mother today." A technician increases the Doctor's interdependence.

The Doctor adjusts his stance and then states emphatically, "You Americans with your guns and hamburgers." The speech erupts from the Doctor's mouth overlaid with distortion and reverberation. Someone comments, "He always talked fast."

The Doctor says, "Hello." Then follows up with, "Si." Then, "Say again." Rasmussen addresses the agent, "Dr. Perez." Dr. Perez responds with, "We need to help them. TOO-DAY." The last word is distorted and elongated as he speaks.

The camera sweeps past white hospital curtains lined up against the back wall of the triage room. The edges of the curtains are shredded and splattered with blood. Rasmussen says to the project manager: "Excuse everyone. We need to spend time debugging." Rasmussen continues: "There are two big demos next week. General Willis is coming through. He should be treated with deference. He has more influence than anybody." Most of the audience leaves, while a few remain for the debugging session.

Face as Representation

The rhetoric of ICT research depends on conventional notions of verisimilitude and transparency (in stark contrast to the earlier cartoon iteration of Steve). Verisimilitude is a goal for each of the ICT simulations in that a concept of realism—a mapping of the way in which the world works—is designed and rendered into each scenario. The movement and responses of each virtual human and the supporting cast of characters (who populate the scenes and operate on a loop) are developed so as to replicate photographic motion picture visuality (which is, of course, distinct from notions one may have regarding the "reality" of daily life).

Transparency serves as a complementary goal to verisimilitude in that the user should not have to learn to play the simulation, but should be able to readily understand the way the interface works and simply perceive it as a window onto a world. This world must respond in both its physics and social psychology as if it were grounded in everyday experience. However, the technical glitches and limits on computer processing power at the time that the demonstrations were held served to disrupt the transparency of the user's interactions with the virtual humans (a great deal of processing power was dedicated to the voice recognition portion of MRE and SASO-ST, while rendering the world and animating the characters also demanded considerable computer resources). Under these technological constraints, the idea of seamless transparency remained a distant promise (and to some extent still does). As such the MRE and SASO-ST simulations necessarily represent to the user a garbled set of communication transparencies and a distorted form of verisimilitude.

But it is not simply the flak generated by the deficiencies of technology that undermine the intentions of the ICT designers and their Army backers; rather, it is the continuity of unexamined assumptions through which the ICT virtual humans developed over a series of simulations that causes concern. As social theorist Donna Haraway suggests, "Technologies and scientific discourses can be partially understood as formalizations, i.e., as frozen moments, of the fluid social interactions constituting them, but they should also be viewed as instruments for enforcing meanings."[15] In other words, the virtual human agent system is a record of the "fluid social interactions" that arise between the ICT designers and military cultures, and is an "instrument for enforcing meanings" upon the user of the training system.

New media theorist Lev Manovich emphasizes that there are forms of interactivity beyond what he calls "operational interactivity." Although specifically addressing the formal and narrative aspects of new media (defined broadly, but concentrating mostly on interactive art and digital cinema), Manovich's nuanced view of interaction is pertinent to understanding the interactivity built into the virtual agent systems at the ICT. Manovich states:

> When we use the concept of "interactive media" exclusively in relation to computer-based media, there is the danger that we will interpret "interaction" literally, equating it with physical interaction between a user and a media object (pressing a button, choosing a link, moving the body), at the expense of psychological interaction. The psychological processes of filling-in, hypothesis formation, recall, and identification, which are required for us to comprehend any text or image at all, are mistakenly identified with an objectively existing structure of interactive links.[16]

While ICT simulations are troubled by their lack of functionality—at the level of button-pushing, link-choosing, body-moving as Manovich would have it—the psychological interactivity that Manovich describes is also hindered by the discrepancies in modeling the behaviors and emotions of their virtual agents. For users to believe in narratives about the world—in the psychologically complex ways that are commonly brought to novels and cinema—then the social and cultural cues that shape most interpersonal communication must be fluid and transparent. Through the branching structures of the MRE and SASO-ST narratives, while relying on Hollywood notions of storytelling for dramatic conflict, each of the characters, intelligent agent or otherwise, functions as a proposition about the nature of human interaction. Game studies scholar Phoebe Sengers suggests: "If humans understand intentional behavior by organizing it into narrative, then our agents will be more 'intentionally comprehensible' if they provide narrative cues."[17] Unfortunately, these interactions for the ICT are heavily coded through the typical telegraphic characterizations embedded in most Hollywood films and broadcast media.[18]

Dr. Perez represents a Spanish doctor working in Iraq. His accent is thick, although this is difficult to say for certain due to the audio distortion that masked his voice during the test. This attempt at giving the agent an ethnic identity derives from the narrative scenario and alters the presence that the agent brings to the screen. In the earlier versions of the ICT simulations built around STEVE, which relied on politeness and coaching as a model for human interaction, the Dr. Perez computer architecture has been reworked from scratch and intends to present the user with an agent possessed of a more confrontational demeanor. As such, Dr. Perez exhibits a more complicated relationship with the user, embodied within the SASO-ST scenario as the Captain. There is a differential in power between the Captain and Dr. Perez and the intentions of each are at odds with the other. In the test described above, Dr. Perez begins the interaction with a telling bodily act of defiance by folding his arms across his chest. While Dr. Perez can barter and negotiate with the Captain, power ultimately resides with the user. If Dr. Perez fails to comply and move his hospital, with or without the help of the U.S. Army, his location will be bombed in the days to come. The implied narrative is that many casualties will result and Dr. Perez will be at fault (although, surely the blame would fall on the Army if it were to happen). Obviously, the training goal here is for the Captain (i.e., the user) to make sure that this tragedy does not occur, but the implication is that Dr. Perez is idealistic and manipulative, wanting to leverage the situation to maximize the benefit to his hospital, and is therefore reticent to simply comply with the Captain's entreaties to move.

In addition, the overall visual realization of the SASO-ST scenario provides the user with a grim reminder of war while displacing the consequences. Those people who caused the man to lose his limbs or the girl to lose her parents are never named. Within the logic of the SASO-ST scenario, the U.S. Army could have as easily been at fault, as could have Iraqi insurgents (though we must presume, following the logic of military funding, that this is not so). What remains, though, is a dynamic of facial representation that codes the world of each simulation as a binary, in effect compressing the possibilities inherent in most real world experiences, between a polite and helpful military and an obstinate and, at times, aggressive antagonist. It is no small matter that the conflict in the SASO-ST scenario is coded around ethnic "Otherness" to boot.[19]

Embodiment: The Quantification of the Pedagogical Self

In the ICT promotional video and the troubleshooting sessions that I observed, ICT researchers emphasized the range of emotional content that had been programmed into their virtual humans. Every user interaction with an intelligent agent generated a response on the part of the agent that was colored, or inflected, with differing degrees of emotional intensity on a numerical scale. As demonstrated in the SASO-ST test, the programmer overseeing a simulation could alter a simple slider on each scale for a set of emotional characteristics—joy, anger, shame, and such—giving the agent an interactive agenda that developed from the total emotional setting selected at a given moment. Each adjustment of a slider resulted in a change in the demeanor of the agent. Whereas the agent may have been reacting passively to the user, after a change in emotional content the agent began to disagree and to suggest more aggressively alternate paths to his or her goal as defined by the simulation's training requirements. However, while the promotional materials boasted an infinite range and variety of emotional responses on the part of an agent, in practice, the agent's emotional possibilities at this stage of technological realization remained limited.

Regardless of the actual functionality of the agents and their emotional states in the technological configurations at the ICT, the idea that one can quantify human emotions through adjustments in numerical sliders may seem resonant with the many dystopian futures depicted in science fiction literature and cinema (in ways that are in line with similar anxieties that surround teaching machines as discussed in chapter 2). People for the most part hold firm to the idea that complex emotion, as much as cognition, separates humans from animals and robots.[20] Of course, this may stem as much from residual aspects of a lingering romanticism as it does from reliable fears of industrial production and consumption. But this resistance to quantification, at least at this juncture, does have an empirical basis. As cognitive scientist Richard Lazarus notes:

> An emotional encounter is not a single action or reaction, as in a still photo or a static stimulus-response unit, but a continuous flow of actions and reactions among the persons who participate in it. This flow can generate new emotions or lead to changes in earlier ones. It is usually an action of some sort that precipitates an emotion sequence. We might call the action the provocation of the emotion.[21]

What Lazarus is claiming here is that human emotion works on a biological and conceptual level in ways that are more akin to an analog system than to one that is defined as digital. And, of course, what the sliders represent in SASO-ST is a digital system that samples the range of possible emotions available to the agent as its interaction with the human user progresses. As in digital music where the appearance, a digital sampling, of the available frequency range substitutes for the actual dynamic range of original source sound, the ICT researchers suggest that, contrary to Lazarus's conception of emotion as flow, what appears to us as nuances of emotion can be transcribed to a numerical scale composed of discrete units of intensity.

Trained musicians claim that digital sound, composed of a quantified approximation of the sound waves that exist in the world of performance prior to recording, lacks the richness of both the original sound delivered by the orchestral instruments and the analog sound of tape or vinyl recordings. Now, the privileging or preferencing of one type of sound over another may be a result of a nostalgic longing for the recorded sound with which one is familiar, but nevertheless the sound on a digital recording is qualitatively distinct from one recorded on analog equipment. Moreover, most untrained ears can hear this difference if digital and analog recordings are played one after another.[22]

On the other hand, Rasmussen and the ICT researchers argued at the time of the tests that as the technology improves, the emotional representation through quantification would better reflect the finite, yet finely nuanced, range of human affective responses to situations. They claimed, and rightly so, that their work was moving toward a greater verisimilitude as the technology and science improved. And while the stutters in voice recognition, pauses in movement, and strangely vacant expressions of the crop of virtual humans that I observed failed to capture the distinct attributes of living human beings, in the near future, according to Rasmussen, these troublesome quirks will drop away in the wake of further technological innovations.[23]

Consequently, our predilection for reading all gestures and responses as emotionally resonant and representative of an agent's emotional state at a given moment will no longer be a problem as agent response time accelerates with increases in computer processing speed and algorithms of emotion that allow witty comments and facial expressions to match those of the human-user. According to this line of thinking, the current dissonance between expected human response and simulated agent gesture will no longer exist. Lazarus, whose work has been influential with Rasmussen in particular, argues this very point:

> Even the absence of an action when it is expected or desired can be a provocation, as when we want another person to do something, such as give a gift or an opinion, express appreciation (gratitude) for a gift, or pay a compliment. However, in this case, the other person waits for the action in vain, which is what provokes an emotion, such as disappointment, anger, anxiety, or guilt.[24]

Lazarus's comments highlight one of the key weaknesses of both the MRE and SASO-ST tests. But Rasmussen observes that an agent's emotional response need not correspond with the actual emotional interactions being comprehended by a human-user. Instead, it only matters that the agent *appears* to speak and act using the appropriate emotional representation of what a human-user believes is appropriate for a given situation.[25] This is a version, based on emotional attributes, of the famous Turing test for artificial intelligence in which a user interacts with another entity whose identity is unknown to the user. If the user is incapable of determining whether the entity is human or machine then for all intents and purposes the unseen entity is deemed intelligent by human standards.[26]

Anthropologist Lucy Suchman describes one of the more famous versions of Turing's idea employed in an early AI system called DOCTOR (developed by the late MIT researcher Joseph Weizenbaum). DOCTOR relies on what she refers to, referencing sociologist Karl Mannheim, as the "documentary method of interpretation." The DOCTOR program engages users by asking for generalized information regarding whatever psychological problems they are facing and then repeats back verbatim parts of their reply.[27] "Very simply the documentary method refers to the observation that people take appearances as evidence for, or document of, an ascribed underlying reality, while taking the reality so ascribed as a resource for the interpretation of the appearance."[28] Thus, the appearance of intelligence allows the user to believe that the more complicated processes that normally underlie intelligence are at work behind the formal attributes being displayed by an agent system. Emotion is likewise assumed by a user to have a depth of meaning generating the display that characterizes a given emotion; for example, tears as a signifier for sadness and such.[29]

For the ICT pedagogical agents, this appearance of emotional content results from the quantification of affect as observed through human interaction. Thus the precondition is set for an experience of embodiment on the part of the learner-user. Each slider panel and numerical value serves to indicate intensities of emotion regardless of the causal incident or meaning from which an emotion event ensued. This particular approach to quantifying an area of human experience that previously relied on qualitative or intuitive explanations evokes the similar calculations during the nineteenth century by those researchers who sought to create a science of vision. Art historian Jonathan Crary notes:

> Vision, as well as the other senses, is now describable in terms of abstract and exchangeable magnitudes. If vision previously had been conceived as an experience of qualities (as in Goethe's optics), it is now a question of differences in quantities, of sensory experience that is stronger or weaker. But this new valuation of perception, this obliteration of the qualitative in sensation through its arithmetical homogenization, is a crucial part of modernization.[30]

This method of thinking about vision disregarded the meaning that adheres to specific events and interactions, and replaced them with a focus on intensities and aggregates. This same reconceptualizing holds true for what the ICT researchers are trying to accomplish with emotion. The implications for this research agenda—the replacement of what we perceive as human emotional content with the appearance of this same content—returns us to the ethical dilemma posed by *Ender's Game*.

While the intentions of the ICT researchers and designers are more benign than those that drove the military brass on Ender's earth (attempting to provide military officers with the necessary interpersonal, cross-cultural training versus destroying an entire alien civilization), it remains that the simulation of emotion and cognition can have consequences in the actual world in which combat occurs. The ethics involved in developing simulations for combat training invoke other aspects of Card's science fiction parable as well. As one officer who attended the SASO-ST test suggested to me, he would like to run reconnaissance in the morning, design the simulation in the afternoon, and deploy his troops in the evening. While this goal is highly plausible, it ignores the larger cultural issues surrounding the ability of the designers to design for the actuality of combat as it may or may not "play" on the ground. And as this play is dependent on the multitude of variables available to simulation designers drawn from field reconnaissance—the validity of which is always in doubt—it suggests that a perfect correspondence between what is present in the field and what can be represented on the screen is a quixotic goal at best.

Furthermore, human communication in real time through corporeal bodily gesture, facial expression, odor, skin texture, clothing, and voice currently trumps all of the electronic and digital technologies of embodiment that are available to the designers of AI versions of pedagogical agents. Yet this does not mean that increased technological sophistication, call it greater "bandwidth," will not someday provide users with experiences comparable to today's face-to-face forms of human communication (or the enthusiasms exuded by a beloved teacher). By the standards of human communication and expressivity considered the benchmark by most people (communication taking place in the presence of others), all of the mediated forms of communication are lacking, but there seems to be little consensus as to what exactly is lacking. Is it the warmth of touch, the physicality of another's body, or is it any of the myriad other communication channels available to those who are seated across from one another sipping a cappuccino? All of these "channels," value added attributes of face-to-face interaction, signal a horizon that delimits the extent to which simulation can stand in for direct human communication in an educational context. Gazing at that horizon, it becomes easy to perceive the folly of romanticism by clinging to the "human" as the baseline for all interaction, but also the bracing chill of instrumental reason, the "cost-benefit, means-ends thinking of engineers" (and the military), as it plays out in *Ender's Game*. At this juncture in technological development, the teacher-embodied mode signals a split between what many fear the most—loss of presence in the face of new media and technologies—and what others hope will be the answer to the need for satisfying and sustaining pedagogical and communicative interactions across distances and time.

CONCLUSION

Presence, Telepresence, and the Gift of Pedagogy

But when from a long-distant past nothing subsists, after the people are
dead, after the things are broken and scattered, taste and smell alone,
more fragile but more enduring, more immaterial, more persistent, more
faithful, remain poised a long time, like souls, remembering, waiting,
hoping, amid the ruins of all the rest; and bear unflinchingly, in the
tiny and almost impalpable drop of their essence, the vast structure of
recollection.

—Marcel Proust, *In Search of Lost Time*[1]

In the 1939 film *Goodbye Mr. Chips*, a short montage sequence depicts a suc-
cession of English lads arriving each fall at Brookfield boarding school. The
sequence suggests the passage of time as the world changes around the aging
master of classical studies, Mr. Chipping (Robert Donat). Chips, as his wife
affectionately calls him, mentors class after class of schoolboys through a combination of encyclopedic knowledge, pleasant enthusiasm, and fatherly affec-
tion. At times doddering, and as frayed as the gown which flows behind him
like a disheveled superhero's cape as he hurries from classroom to classroom,
Mr. Chips personifies the figure of the beloved teacher. Of course, upon reflection, it is apparent that this figure of the befuddled and beloved teacher was
already nostalgic and slightly musty at the time of the film's production (glance
at the soft glow of the mise-en-scène, listen to the treacly music). But Chips
distills, in fictional form, a grandly imagined moment in the popular conception of the teacher as the figure who shapes pedagogy through presence.

The Distance, the Interval

The ugly philosopher Socrates, Plato's voice within the text of his dialogue *Pha-edrus*, condemns writing as a technology that displaces the authentic knowledge gained through direct engagement with a teacher. As evidence, Socrates recalls the story of King Thamus who ruled over Ancient Egypt and confronted the god Thoth at the introduction of writing into the kingdom:

> Thanks to you and your invention [writing], your pupils will be widely read without the benefit of a teacher's instruction; in consequence, they'll entertain the delusion that they have wide knowledge, while they are, in fact, for the most part incapable of real judgment. They will also be difficult to get on with since they will have become wise merely in their own conceit, not genuinely so.[2]

For Plato, as for Socrates (and, presumably, Thamus), writing gives to students an illusory form of knowledge by allowing them to depend on a prosthetic mnemonic device, the text. Written texts serve as repositories of thought and action (as description, analysis, and narrative) distant from their source in the mind or speech of the teacher and therefore they weaken the practice of memory (and consequently attention) which serves as the primary mental faculty necessary for learning. Under this line of reasoning, memory is vital for cultivating judgment as it resides within the body of a teacher or student and is thus constitutive of action in the form of dialogue. Consequently, writing as a prosthesis of memory, replacing the more rigorous memory individual to each student, encourages partial and slovenly forms of learning to occur through the absence of an exacting mentor (as Socrates must have been). The need for the ongoing presence of the teacher as interlocutor, immediate in the flesh, lies at the heart of Plato's critique of writing as a technology as much as it justifies his program for pedagogy (which is at the service of his philosophy).

But for others in the Western tradition, always grappling with the ongoing influence of Plato's ideas, books as archives of human thought suggested a positive break with the potential tyranny of the schoolmaster (or church).[3] The Protestant Reformation's break with the Catholic Church as arbiter of the word of God opened up the possibility that literacy, privately read texts, could generate knowledge—possibly subversive, possibly sublime—that contradicted tradition and ideology (embodied by the tutor as much as by the priest). The gatekeeping role of the teacher as sole sculptor of the contours of knowledge—as seen in the public roles of the lector and the scholar—remained in force even as radical and liberal thought circulated throughout Europe and America during the Enlightenment, and afterwards, in the form of commonplace books, pamphlets, and samizdat. Contrary to Plato's warning, writing made possible the transmission of knowledge through a mediated form of presence—a form that was most fully explored in the literary genres of the memoir and the novel.

By moving the space of memory away from the flesh-brain, written texts distanced knowledge from the ephemera of the body while acknowledging the never-stilling oscillation of presence and absence that determines the relationship between knower and communicator (which in the body and voice of the teacher are collapsed into one). Transmitting knowledge no longer relied on another living human being—a being which brought with it warmth, admonishment, influence, passion, hatred, love (an affective summary of the beloved teacher)—but instead demanded that the seemingly inert words on the page be reactivated during reading. Consequently, reading brought forth the absent communicator as a stream of thought from the past made present, but it also activated, through the muteness of absence, the possibility that knowledge without presence can lead to misreading, miscommunication, and deception (which can have both destructive and creative results). Therefore, texts as archives of thought, memory vaults, transformed the social relations of modernity—a process in which Plato, through his written dialogues, had a hand—as newer and newer technologies were relentlessly introduced, as a result of industrial production and the flows of capital, into cultural, pedagogical, and commercial spaces since at least the late nineteenth century.

In an argument that echoes Plato, urban theorist Paul Virilio (who has written extensively on the historical developments that link mechanized warfare, "vision machines," and human perception) [4] notes:

> Since the nineteenth century, the muscular force of the human being is literally "laid off" when automation of the "machine tool" is employed. Then, with the recent growth of computers, "transmission machines," comes the laying off or ultimate shutdown of human memory and conscience.... Thus the interface in real time definitely replaces the interval that had formerly constructed and organized the history and geography of our societies.[5]

For Virilio this change in interface signals the moment at which, through the effects of speed on human perception and thought, the reflective element of human cognition (derived from experience) is replaced by a reactive form of machine cognition that supersedes morality. Virilio's position, like that of Plato and most critics of technology, is fundamentally an argument grounded in judgments regarding the value of the human over that of the machine (or prosthetic technologies in general). Human memory and reflection as occurring in a state of existence free of machine intervention and interface—an Eden of pretechnological innocence—stand for Virilio (though he writes with a particularly contemporary wit and sarcasm alien to Plato) as the mark of what it means to be human. To displace human thought and reflection with a cognitive prosthesis, a thinking machine, represents the original sin that cast our society out of its preindustrial garden. For Plato that moment was the introduction of writing; for Virilio that moment happens with the introduction of remote sensing and simulation technologies. Like the text, the screen pushes away the human, elides presence, and thus corrupts the real time morality of the living human being. Whereas the text archives memory, the technological interval, the distance between judgment and action, signals a loss of presence that can only lead to physical and moral disaster.

While Virilio represents perhaps the most exaggerated vision of the corruption of the human by technology (with Plato representing the oldest), there are other media theorists who provide more nuanced, or more ambivalent, arguments on the loss of human presence in the shadow of the machine. German media theorist Friedrich Kittler suggests that a key transformation in notions of presence occurred with the introduction of the typewriter in the late nineteenth century, as this machine gained prominence as the standard method for composing text and correspondence. "To mechanize writing, our culture had to redefine its values or (as the German monograph on the typewriter put it, in anticipation of Foucault) 'create a wholly new order of things.'"[6] Whereas once writing constituted an analogical record of the hand of the writer (much as the vinyl grooves of the LP record album traced the sine wave of the music performed), with the introduction of the typewriter, a digital form of writing became commonplace. The signature of the author, presence traced through ink on the page, was now hidden by a mechanical typeface, effectively erasing the materiality of the body. While the typewriter provided for new forms of value associated with efficiency and economy (a "new order of things") it simultaneously set about displacing another set of values that had for years grounded a whole cultural sphere. With the coming of the personal computer this transformation is, discounting romantics and eccentrics who write with fountain pens and ballpoints, all but complete.[7] On Kittler's point, the scratch (noise) and the tooth (touch) that comes when applying pen nib and ink to rag paper could substitute for Proust's madeleine triggering the "vast structure of recollection."

This material presence through digitalization, the signature of the self, hidden by the keystrokes of the typewriter, underscores much of what has been said by the ICT researchers regarding the attempts at programming human emotion. Is the loss of the affective quality of human presence through technological mediation merely a problem of what Larry Rasmussen refers to as "bandwidth?" As he suggested in reference to the ICT virtual human simulations, the "bandwidth" in human-to-human communication continues to be many times greater than that available in even the most advanced broadband network. If the bandwidth of human communication, the fully present human during interaction, can be envisioned as the summative total of communicative action between two participants—the nuanced gestures, spoken language, body positions, nonverbal utterances, touch, smell and taste, and clothing and hairstyle—then it follows that there may be a limit to the transparency of mediated communication as it materially represents a diminished, and therefore more impoverished, bandwidth (at least for the near future). Put simply, the signatures of human presence, the materiality of what it means to be human, sink deep into the cultural and social context of communication and demand that the technological interface produce a performance of presence in excess of the necessary cognitive and informational content. Therefore, presence is not necessarily summative of, but, rather, supplemental to the semiotic system that is human communicative interaction.

Face-to-face presence can be understood as much by its being embedded in a set of psychological, social, and cultural interactions, bounded by the habits of daily life, as by its apparent loss with the onslaught of mediation using screens on cell phones, televisions, or computers. Film theorist Vivian Sobchack, drawing upon the work of Heidegger, reminds those technological determinists who fret over the lack of bandwidth in relation to mediation that:

> Technology…is historically informed not only by its materiality but also by its political, economic, and social context, and thus it both co-constitutes and expresses not merely technological value but always also cultural values.[8]

Thus, presence as produced through technology gains value not only from the increasing verisimilitude of its representations (bandwidth, cost, interactive transparency), but also from its use of culturally determined forms of human affect and cognition (innocence, authenticity, reality, and faith). While it is crucial to understand presence as a blunt material condition of human communication (the mass of the body, the heat of existence), it is also important to look at the cultural indicators that divide the artificial, the copy, from the human, the original.

But there is an important distinction that arises at this point. Is presence as a cultural form related to signal, the content of interaction, or to noise, the interruptions and confusions that disrupt transparency? Researcher Claude Shannon suggested in his pioneering work on communication theory that information as the content of a message should be seen in contrast to the noise that is inherent to any medium of transmission (in his case, the telephone). In his theory, the signal containing a message should be of sufficient strength so that the noise (the distortion of the signal) within the medium will not obliterate the information being sent.[9] An obvious example of this is what is called the signal-to-noise ratio in television and video engineering. The video signal transmitting the image of an evening news anchorperson must be at a level of intensity greater than the noise (which is called "snow" in industry parlance) present in the broadcast system. To see the noise in the system, in its purest form, a viewer must simply turn to a dead channel (a rarity these days with round-the-clock broadcast and cable networks). The flurry of snowlike particles swirling across the picture on the dead channel represents the zero-degree signal of the transmission medium. What this explanation highlights is that noise is present as a background to any given signal such as muffled voices, video snow, or visual distractions, but the point that is often missed in Shannon's theory is that noise is a positive attribute of the system as well. Noise is a matter of the viewer's perspective defined by the assumptions that he or she brings to the interaction enabled by the communication system. What is a given viewer's tolerance when considering the noise versus the signal? How much is the viewer willing to interpret or supplement the message, to fill in the gaps, using experience and judgment as a guide, in relation to what is missing? It depends on what information the viewer holds as being critical to an understanding of a given communicative event.

The notion of bandwidth mentioned by the ICT researchers suggests that there is a quantitative value at which the signal overcomes the noise, or is able to stand out from the noise, and thus a perceptually transparent human communicative interaction takes place (one in which the functionality of the technological medium disappears in deference to the actuality of human interaction). But, what the above discussion of noise as an inherent part of the perceptual understanding of a medium suggests is that perhaps human presence, rather than being the signal of communication, and by extension, pedagogy, is instead a form of noise in human interaction (as a positive form of information as well as a negative) and needs to be reassigned a lesser perceptual weight for mediated presence to be effectively realized. Reeves and Nass's research on the media equation and Sherry Turkle's work from the 1990s on online identity[10] seem to back up a conclusion that human–machine interaction derives from a set of habituated routines built upon daily experience with humans and objects. Thus, human users feel the need to assign to objects the affective and cognitive attributes that are in many instances on a par with those assigned to humans even when the reciprocating communication from the device suggests that the problems or successes of a given interaction with technology are related to programming, design, or accident. For example, we curse at our laptop when the battery has simply stopped working (or colloquially, "the computer has died").

While the ICT researchers imagine, and depend on, a future moment when bandwidth within their simulations more closely matches the information capacity of daily human interaction, the technology necessary to represent even an approximate version of the verisimilitude of daily life, a transparent reality as such, seems elusive. The limitations of the virtual humans in the ICT troubleshooting sessions—remembering that they were "advanced" research projects and therefore the state of the art in their field at the time—begin to sketch in the type of technological innovations that this kind of performative realism will require. There may come a time when everyday technologies will be able to reproduce the texture of Mr. Tamberlin's jacket or the smell of his musky cologne, but even this kind of reproductive fidelity may not be sufficient to embody or represent the totality of his presence, that material essence, a culmination of many sensations buried in my memory, which can summon forth the fullness of his being-in-the-flesh encountered all those years ago.

Pedagogy as a key component of what it means to communicate (the transmission of thought across generations) and to be human, as opposed to animal or machine, is most often grounded in the notion of presence and to a great extent depends upon the functional attributes of presence to serve its communicative core. The existence of the beloved teacher is framed through this notion of presence. *Goodbye Mr. Chips*, as a narrative of pedagogy, depends on the copresence of Chips and his students. But does this narrative of copresence, based on the comfort and fullness of the other, merely result from the familiarity of living in, until recently, the exclusively bodied world of the flesh?

If I try to stick my hand into the screen of my computer—a vision that is played out in many science fiction narratives, most explicitly in David Cronenberg's film *Videodrome* (1983)—it will not reward my touch with tactile pleasure but instead rebuffs my need to connect: A slap of glass on my wrist, so to speak. In contrast, it seems that as I sit lazily thumbing through a book on a sweltering afternoon, my interpenetration of the material object, cultural and historical thoughts aside, is more visceral, more real. I feel the texture of the paper, my eyes discern the slightly ragged edges of the printed type, my ear catches the crack of the cheap glue that binds the pages, my sweat drops onto the page and is soaked up momentarily. My mind is engaged with thinking and reflecting and feeling, as is my body. A cool draft of nostalgia for the presence of that hot afternoon in the late 1960s overtakes me. But my memory serves this thought: presence may simply be a residual nostalgia that is felt by bodies as a matter of habit. Communication and pedagogy may be habitually located in presence, but this need for presence will be necessarily displaced as the need for other forms of interaction come into play: forms of interaction that rely on a greater technological fidelity than is possible at this historical juncture; forms of interaction that will build new habits and new forms of nostalgia—telepresence. One day telepresence may stand in relation to human interaction in many, if not all of the ways through the amnesia of social consensus, that face-to-face presence once served. Something will be lost, but not remembered in any event, so not lost actually. Telepresence, the communication of mediated humans, may simply be called "presence."

Speaking, or the Unexpected Question

As the materiality of bodies and objects define pedagogical presence, speech provides the Janus-faced complementary component to the experience of pedagogical presence. Speech, the voice of the lecturer and the interlocutor, stands as the medium upon which education depends (as it does in the most pedagogical of mainstream media forms, the documentary). This dependence on the voice reduces the immediacy of the touch, smell, and sight of the teacher and renders these other sensations as supplemental (but as said throughout, not inconsequential). Thus, the voice becomes the primary medium of instruction (allied with the body and the screen as discussed in chapter 2). Often in educational theory, pedagogical speech is divided into those forms that center on direct address (the lecture and the drill) and those that focus on dialogue (conversation and discussion).

In progressive education and critical pedagogy, dialogue is privileged over the lecture, as it has been implicitly and explicitly throughout *Teaching with the Screen*. For example, educational theorist Ivan Illich contrasts "humane education" with "skill instruction" (a designation which recalls many of the points put forth by B. F. Skinner in relation to teaching machines):

> Most skills can be acquired and improved by drills, because skill implies the mastery of definable and predictable behavior. Skill instruction can rely, therefore, on the simulation of circumstances in which the skill will be used.... [Humane] education can be the outcome of instruction, though instruction of a kind fundamentally opposed to drill. It relies on the relationship between partners who already have some of the keys which give access to memories stored in and by the community. It relies on the critical intent of all those who use memories creatively. It relies on the surprise of the unexpected question which opens new doors for the inquirer and his partner.[11]

Thus skills are a set of closed determinants on the instruction at hand, presupposing drill and lecture, while education proper is an open-ended dialogical process that by intention eschews predictable results. This lack of predictability, inherent in dialogic interaction, is obviously at odds with the increasingly managerial notion of information access and acquisition that structures the organization of knowledge in contemporary society (and infuses the work of Capretz and the ICT researchers). Skills instruction as lecture and drill (with a feedback performance evaluation built into the teaching machine) can serve an accelerating perceptual time-space (a dromological society as Virilio would have it) as a form of "speed" instruction where a group of easily defined skills is acquired in the shortest period of time with no room for extended exploration of more complex topics.[12]

On the other hand, humane education as envisioned by Illich counters this notion of efficiency of resources and is time intensive, based on dialogue, and uncertain in outcome. This uncertainty, though, with its greater reliance on reflective forms of thinking should lead, at least in Illich's conception, to more innovative approaches to solving problems that arise in the public spheres outside schooling (inclusive of political, social, cultural, aesthetic, and economic concerns) and allows ultimately for the possibility of increased rewards for the schooled as well (in contrast to speed-intensive learning which demands reactive thinking and consequently surrenders innovation to the tried-and-true).

But with this possibility of a larger pay-off—in the form of innovation *and* critical reflection—also comes an increased likelihood of failure (as failure is the constant in experimentation, success the exception) in either the production or application of knowledge generated through open-ended educational encounters. For Illich, the technique of humane education demands dialogue as a method of inquiry while the technique of skills instruction demands lecture and drill as a method of knowledge transmission. Illich's judgment on these matters defines dialogue as a fundamentally more "humane" and thus progressive approach to teaching and learning (in line with the emphasis placed on dialogue by those in progressive education and critical pedagogy mentioned above).

But new media theorist Vilém Flusser's distinction between discourse and dialogue brings additional nuance to Illich's dichotomy:

> In discourse, information is contained in the memory of the sender and transmitted to the memory of the receiver ... an example of this is a lecture. In dialogue, there is partial information in the memories of the participants that is being synthesized into global information by the process ... an example of this is parliamentary debate that elaborates a law. The dynamic of communication is the elaboration of information through dialogue and its transmission through discourse.[13]

Therefore, for Flusser, information, an accumulation of knowledge that exists prior to the body of the teacher or communicator, precedes the transmission of information through discourse, but becomes transformed during the more generative process of dialogue. The lecture (or in a more fragmentary manner, the drill) remains an efficient method of transmission of information, skills, and accumulated knowledge, but the creation of new knowledge depends on reciprocal interaction between individuals and groups to occur. The scene of each of these forms of communication—the situation that guides the outcomes desired—determines the uses to which each, dialogue or discourse, can be put.

To further complicate Illich's seemingly simple dichotomy, communication theorist John Durham Peters argues against the notion held by many educators and scholars that one-way communication, what he calls dissemination, should be regarded as a degraded form of communication while dialogue should be privileged as inherently more democratic.[14] Through an examination of Socrates as the exemplary practitioner of dialogue and Jesus as the exemplar for dissemination (both of whom, in line with Dewey's comment on all communication being educative, are often seen as models of teaching), Peters makes the case for the situational efficacy of dissemination as an approach to communication. Just as in some instances the process of dialogue can provide for a more open field of inquiry, dissemination can in other instances provide for a more democratic form of communication when a message is intended for a larger audience—a multitude in the case of the Gospels. In dissemination, the seed of the idea is given over to the audience who then is allowed to make of it what they will, while in contrast dialogue can follow a path leading to coercion and a demand of fealty to an acknowledged leader (whether determined through charisma, institutional hierarchy, or group dynamics). Jesus in his sermons asks his audience to understand as he does, yet the condition of understanding remains with the audience member and the direction of revelation remains potentially a crooked path. Peters does not want to undermine the value of dialogue, but he does want to upset the conventionalized notion, fostered by those such as Illich, that dialogue is inherently more democratic and valuable than dissemination. Peters, like Flusser, recognizes that each form of communication, dialogue and discourse (dissemination), has a context in which it is most productive (and most humane).

Thus, acknowledging that dissemination and dialogue both have a place in the transmission and generation of knowledge, Illich's dichotomy suggests a return to Skinner's notion of programmed instruction that cedes the more routine aspects of education to machines that excel at repetition and standardization. Echoing Skinner (but under renewed conditions pertaining to late twentieth century forms of technology and educational organization), communication theorist Hans Ulrich Gumbrecht notes:

> There cannot be any doubt that most of the classes strictly limited to the transmission of standard knowledge will—and should—soon be replaced by a variety of technological devices that do not require the physical co-presence of students and teachers.[15]

The material realities of transmission, in effect turning Freire's critique of the banking concept of education on its head, suggest that teaching machines (necessarily lacking the affective qualities of the human) can be the most effective means of skill instruction (for instance, the numerous computer programs that mimic flash cards) and can indeed replace the flesh-and-blood teacher as the sole presence in the instructional moment (presence bleeds away in the face of the blunt repetition of the rigorous machine). But, before we consign all undergraduates in the lecture hall to robot instruction and become complicit in the campaign to organize education in line with business models, it is important to acknowledge the proper ratio between time spent in school transmitting preexisting information and time spent generating new ideas. Professor Diana Laurillard, an advocate for educational technology, describes what she calls "a conversational framework for learning technologies":

> Given that academic knowledge is a consensual description of experience, it follows that discussion between teachers and students should play a very important part. It should be the mode of learning that drives everything else a student does, even if it is allocated only a small part of the total study time. It should not be vanishingly small, however, and there is an increasing danger that it will be.[16]

But this ratio between transmission and inquiry should acknowledge as well Illich's notion of the unexpected question. In a cost-benefit analysis of mainstream pedagogy, most aptly identified with the large lecture hall, the unexpected question can seem like a nuisance (and would most likely be seen as such in all of the educational settings described in my case studies). However, it also remains important to situate this form of inquiry, from out of the blue so to speak, as a way to problematize the routine production of pedagogy. Illich speaks to this when he calls the pedagogic act a form of "gift" from one human being to another:

> Aristotle speaks of it as a "moral type of friendship, which is not on fixed terms: it makes a gift, or does whatever it does, as to a friend." Thomas Aquinas says of this kind of teaching that inevitably it is an act of love and mercy. This kind of teaching is always a luxury for the teacher and a form of leisure (in Greek, *"schole"*) for him and his pupil: an activity meaningful for both, having no ulterior purpose.[17]

The language of Illich's idea may sound unduly romantic (or, perhaps, utopian), but his notion of free exchange untroubled by contingencies and economics, or teaching as a gift, attempts to redress the most instrumental aspects of pedagogical agency formulated as an imperative to seek the lowest cost and the most efficient expenditure of time in designing and implementing curriculum. Beware though, Illich's notion of leisure and luxury are not those of a bourgeois subject reclining at the seashore, but rather those of a revolutionary figure standing firm against a barrage of incursions from those who envision education as a form of competition that satisfies the needs of industry. Illich can perhaps be faulted for a neo-utopian outlook (one that was more commonplace in the 1960s and 1970s), but he should not be faulted for emphasizing the participatory relations that form the foundation of teaching as a communal act. While it is important to acknowledge the history of repression and exclusion that has characterized many aspects of education (institutional racism and sexism, symbolic violence, structural discrimination, and such), it is also important to recognize that pedagogy is an act of compassion as much as it is an act of intellect. On this point, Gumbrecht comments:

> Everybody who has ever attended a good university will know what I am talking about and what kind of pedagogical gift I am alluding to. It is the gift, above all, of remaining alert and absolutely open to the others, without falling into the trap of becoming absorbed by their intuitions and positions, and it is the gift of intellectual good taste that stays focused on those very topics that do not allow for quick and easy solutions. Such openness and such focus define the teacher as a catalyst of intellectual events—and I associate the function of the catalyst with the condition of physical presence.[18]

I find compelling his assertion that the complexity of the pedagogical act, at once intensely engaged and consequently erotic, demands that the body of the teacher be present. Or that for teachers to give students something of them-selves demands a "production of presence" (to use Gumbrecht's phrase) in that it demands that the teacher be attentive to all of the sensory cues available in the really existing space of instruction (which discounts most of the pedagogi-cal agents discussed in this text, through their lack of sensory input, regardless of their mode as presented, augmented, or embodied). But this line of inquiry demands an unexpected question on my part voiced to an inattentive audi-ence across the gap that is created by the text as transmitter of disembodied discourse: what if there arises a moment at which all of the preconditions men-tioned by Plato, Virilio, Illich, and Gumbrecht become realized in a technol-ogy that allows for presence to be felt and understood by students in a virtual as opposed to actual space of instruction? What if the preconditions are merely residual in the way that the practice of memory was residual for those prior to the rise of written language? Many pupils will be left out of this newly revised virtual terrain of education, just as those who are "auditory" in their modes of learning are excluded to a great extent by education through the visuality of the book. Many others will simply see the new education, dependent on robots unimagined in our worldviews, as a new habit and will in turn substitute new bodily cues for older ones that once sprang forth so powerfully for Proust when he took a bite from his madeleine.

It is important to acknowledge educational psychologist Jerome Bruner's observation that a technology does not determine the social uses to which it is put. This observation agrees with those made by media historians Raymond Williams[19] and Brian Winston[20] on the development of media in general. The uses develop out of the interrelationship between the user and the existing attributes of that technology as much as they do out of the social and cultural possibilities available to users at each historical moment. While the military and its desire for configurable training simulations drives the programming and design of the current crop of ICT pedagogical agents, at some point certain of these technologies will circulate outwards (accompanied by an industrial and corporate agenda to be sure) for use by those with different, and perhaps more progressive, educational and training goals. At that time, the uses for these screen technologies will be reimagined, and once again pedagogical agency will be renewed.

But it seems safe to assume that the development of advanced learning tech-nologies in the near future will be based on increases in communication trans-parency (in the sense that the media element will not interfere with the process of the real time interaction between teacher and student). Based on the typol-ogy presented in chapter 2, it seems likely that the teacher-presented mode will become increasingly rare as the modalities of fully realized interactive media become an actuality. Interactivity based on mediated presence, even at

the limited level that now occurs during the average college lecture, will dominate as much from the will to do so through the spectacle of technology as from
an ideological need for expression on the part of the student (who most likely
will continue to inhabit the individualized space demarcated by capitalism and
consumer culture). This two-way, one-to-one form of communication can be
embodied by a range of standalone technologies serving as de facto teachers as
much as it can by teachers augmented by a variety of media screens. One can
envision intelligent agent systems that guide one through educational experiences that are not necessarily limited to a rote teaching of skills orientation
(although, as suggested by Illich, this might be the most aptly suited form of
learning for a low-cost agent system).

In this regard, the skills based aspects of any intellectual endeavor, whether
it be a system of logic or a system of analysis, could be reimagined as a journey
in which the learner plays Dante to the intelligent agent's Virgil (to exploit
one classical liberal arts reference to the role of the teacher in relation to the
student). With attention paid to the more explicitly cultural demands of a given
system (as one does to any other form of creative technology be it film, television, or videogame), a deeply immersive form of instruction that draws on
scenarios similar to those designed for the STEVE simulations should be inevitable, limited only by the social constraints placed on the implementation of
sophisticated teaching machines and the imagination of the designers, artists,
and educators involved.

Similarly, all of the preexisting forms of pedagogy—the lecture, student-
centered instruction, project-work, and such—can also be adapted to the
teacher-augmented mode of screen instruction. But the augmented mode,
while opening up the pedagogical interaction to more fully include students
and screens, still demands that the model of one-to-many communication be
the primary form of delivery. On the other hand, this mode opens up interactive possibilities in the form of dialogues that may engage a community of
learners as opposed to those settings that are dominated by the needs of an individual. It would seem that if one is to envision improved educational methods
that incorporate technology, one must account for both of these forms and consider the particulars of the curricular content, student, and setting to determine
which pedagogical mode is most appropriate.

For the foreseeable future, the categories of teacher presented, augmented,
and embodied can serve as a way to conceptualize the interaction between
teachers, students, and screens/machines (and as a way to emphasize half of
the educational equation, pedagogy, while bracketing learning to one side),
but it seems also that these genres of educational media may need to be revised
or expanded as new technologies come into play. A warning, though, in this
regard: as with Illich's admonition, it is crucial that pedagogy be conceived as
a gift and that the technological interface be conceived of in a like manner; as
a way to foster the gift of teaching and not to incorporate the gift as simply

one more commodity to be technologized and sold to those students who can afford the price. [21]

Therefore, Mr. Chips needs to be reclaimed for the virtual world, after being divested of the gendered nostalgia and authoritarian hierarchy that attaches to his moment in time. He needs to be embodied for a more emancipated population of students and teachers who bring to the educational setting a new, complex set of cultural and ethnic traditions, gendered bodies, creative and destructive impulses, politics, and beliefs and fears. He needs to inhabit the virtual worlds that are being made everyday more real and already more colonized by the pragmatics of corporatism and spectacle that plague the actual world. It is the responsibility of teachers, as much as it is incumbent upon learners, to seize the tools of the digital moment and attempt to reshape the role of the beloved teacher in a way that sustains a reimagined form of pedagogy, as gift and play and technique and art, between teacher, student, and machine.

APPENDIX

How to Teach with Teaching Screens

I have consciously excluded direct statements about the practical approaches to media pedagogy that could result from the theoretical and historical framework that I explore throughout the main text of *Teaching with the Screen*. Nothing becomes stale or soured or goes out of date more quickly than the practical aspects of how to teach with technology. I began my own professional career using a French curve to render ovals for print advertisements and later used Apple's HyperCard and Macromedia's Director programs to craft interactive media for use with high school and college students. While there are transferable skills that I acquired from both of these practical pedagogical experiences, the value of these now-defunct skills is deeply embedded within my own personal and professional history and is not necessarily obvious to the casual observer. Having said that, throughout the research and writing of this book I have thought deeply about the ways in which practical solutions to pedagogical problems could be included.

In the spirit of Sol Lewitt's 1969 *Art-Language* text "Sentences on Conceptual Art," I would like to provide a short list of statements that attempt to suggest heuristics—rules of thumb distilled from the case studies—regarding the best ways to use screens and media technologies in educational settings. Please tear out these pages and tack them to a wall near your classroom or work area (or scan and print so as not to deface this book). Also, please visit my blog (www.teach-screen.org) or follow me on Twitter (@dleopard) and join a discussion about the many ways to teach with screens and media technologies (the list below is certainly not meant to be an exhaustive accounting of the practical concerns associated with critical media pedagogy). Or start a discussion about other topics of interest that have occurred to you as you read this book. Visit: www.teach-screen.org or search online for keywords such as "Dan Leopard"

+ "Teaching Screens," "Teaching Machines," "Pedagogical Agents," "Media Education," "Media Pedagogy," and "Critical Media Pedagogy."

Sentences on Critical Media Pedagogy

1. Technology that is of great interest to information technology leaders is often frustrating and irrelevant to the average user.
2. Routine technology is useful technology. Technology that is exceptional resists being functional on a day-to-day basis.
3. Routine uses of technology are the most productive ones. These are not the sexiest approaches to media pedagogy, not those that get you written up in the *New York Times Education Supplement* or the *Chronicle of Higher Education*, but they provide solutions to specific problems of pedagogy.
4. Be a Luddite, but don't throw a wrench into the works.
5. Be skeptical of fads in new media and educational technology, especially when sponsored by someone with an incentive to sell you hardware or software.
6. However, explore new technologies to see what is possible. Be fearless in this regard.
7. Don't look askance at the experiences of those colleagues who have been around for a while. But, don't give their experience too much credence.
8. Experience as a trump card can block innovation.
9. Remediate, Remediate, Remediate. Media theorist Marshall McLuhan liked to say that society was looking in the rearview mirror as it moved toward the future. Perhaps that is the way it should be. We should use earlier approaches to media-based pedagogy to guide the development of current and future approaches.
10. People think that teaching with media and technology equals a one size fits all approach to instruction. But there are many ways to use media and technology in education.
11. Use media and technology as a form of broadcasting, as dissemination.
12. Use media and technology as a form of social interaction, as dialogue.
13. Use media and technology as a small-scale production studio.
14. Use the media as a text. Use the technology as a tool.
15. As human-created objects, the design of specific software and hardware configures the ways in which technology can be used as a pedagogical tool.
16. The simpler and more flexible the tool, the better.
17. To use media and technology as pedagogical tools, the use of media and technology as a tool must be taught.
18. Consider what each medium brings to the pedagogical arena and what that medium can achieve. An essay in print may be inherently more useful from a pedagogical perspective than a slideshow, video, interactive game, or social media site.

19. Embed media and technology within an instructional framework that includes books and bodies.
20. Prepare for courses by having a plan for technology-based instruction and then a backup plan that involves nothing more than you and your students.
21. Don't romanticize the tech abilities of youth. Dispense with the myth of the "digital natives."
22. Students are essentially no more friendly with technology than their teachers. They merely have more interest, time, and inclination to play and therefore they have mastered the current crop of media.
23. Furthermore, many students have mastered these technologies in ways that do not necessarily produce literacy. They use their chosen technologies along well-trod paths and if requested to leave these beaten paths they are often lost.
24. Those students who use technologies exceptionally well are exceptional students. In the past, these students would have been film monitors. Now they are webmasters.
25. Teachers need to help students use learning technologies in new, unexpected, and rigorous ways. Trust students and clear a space for them to exert their agency.
26. Speak the language of media and popular culture, but don't be a tourist.
27. Search for common ground with students. Overcome distance.
28. Digital literacy is a metaphor. It is not the same as written literacy.
29. Demand a reliable and well-maintained technological infrastructure.
30. Make it open.
31. Be skeptical of corporate sponsorship (it always comes with strings attached).
32. New technologies are ideologies made material in the palm of your hand (or in your backpack, purse, or briefcase).
33. Resist the privatization of education. Education is a public good. It should be treated as such.

These sentences comment on critical pedagogy, but are not critical pedagogy.

NOTES

Introduction

1 Siegfried Kracauer, *The Salaried Masses: Duty and Distraction in Weimer Germany* (London: Verso, 1998), 32.

2 On the notion of cultural consecration as it is used here, see Pierre Bourdieu's work on taste cultures. *Distinction: A Social Critique of the Judgment of Taste*, trans. Richard Nice (Cambridge, MA: Harvard University Press, 1984): "Taste classifies, and it classifies the classifier. Social subjects, classified by their classifications, distinguish themselves by the distinctions they make, between the beautiful and the ugly, the distinguished and the vulgar, in which their position in the objective classifications is expressed or betrayed," and, "Cultural consecration does indeed confer on the objects, persons and situations it touches, a sort of ontological promotion akin to a transubstantiation" (6).

3 Dan C. Lortie, *Schoolteacher: A Sociological Study* (Chicago: University of Chicago Press, 2003), 63–64.

4 Before I sound too utopian, it must be said that the art elective was part of the introductory track for the print communications major at the school. I am sure that his teaching was marginal in the eyes of the math teachers—I seem to recall that Mr. Tamberlin was seen as a "crackpot" by at least one of my algebra teachers—but he did have great influence with students as they began their studies in print media and journalism. Being that I attended a "vocational" school and chose not to enter the college track of elite professions—architecture or mechanical drafting—print communications was actually one of the more prestigious majors available. Our class printed the school newspaper as well as many of the flyers that were distributed by the school administration. We were grunts, but not in the same way that foundry and machine shop kids were.

5 The most famous discussion of this blurring of traditional disciplinary discourse (and methods) belongs to Clifford Geertz in his essay, "Blurred Genres: The Refiguration of Social Thought," in *Local Knowledge: Further Essays in Interpretive Anthropology* (New York: Basic, 1983), 19–35.

6 "Screen theory" is so named for the series of critical interventions that coalesced around the film studies journal *Screen* during the 1970s and 1980s. This densely philosophical and abstracted work is best exemplified by a small selection of benchmark articles that shaped the discourse of film theory during this period. See, for instance, Editorial Collective of *Cahiers*

du Cinéma, "John Ford's Young Mr. Lincoln," *Screen* 13, no. 3 (1972): 5–44; Christian Metz, "The Imaginary Signifier," *Screen* 16, no. 2 (1975): 14–76; and Laura Mulvey, "Visual Pleasure and Narrative Cinema," *Screen* 16, no. 3 (1975): 6–18.

7 In the U.S. context this notion of a transition from an emphasis on production in the media to the consumption of media has been further extended by work on "participatory culture." See, for example, Henry Jenkins, *Convergence Culture: Where Old and New Media Collide* (New York: New York University Press, 2008); and Jean Burgess and Joshua Green, *YouTube: Online Video and Participatory Culture* (Cambridge, UK: Polity, 2009).

8 For plausible overviews of this highly influential work, see, Stuart Hall, Dorothy Hobson, Andrew Lowe, and Paul Willis, eds., *Culture, Media, Language: Working Papers in Cultural Studies, 1972–79* (London: Routledge, 1992) and Graham Turner, *British Cultural Studies: An Introduction* (London: Routledge, 2005). A central influential figure on ethnography in British cultural studies was American sociologist Howard Becker. See Paul Willis, "The Cultural Meaning of Drug Use" for an example of his influence and Geoffrey Pearson and John Twohig, "Ethnography through the Looking-Glass: The Case of Howard Becker" for a critique of Becker's work, both of which are included in Stuart Hall and Tony Jefferson, eds., *Resistance through Rituals: Youth Subcultures in Post-War Britain* (London: Routledge, 1976). For Becker's most famous study of deviance, another form of "studying down," see Howard S. Becker, *Outsiders: Studies in the Sociology of Deviance* (New York: Free Press, 1973).

9 As ethnographer John Van Maanen notes, "Similar to the appeal of open-air anthropology, Chicago-style sociology offered its followers an attractive alternative to the usual survey, documentary, interview, or theory-building work that then marked the discipline.... The urban ethnographers...took to the field not so much for scientific reasons, however, as for more quintessential American ones: Muckraking (to expose the lies and hypocrisies of the Exalted Ones in society) and Reform (to improve the lot of the downtrodden)." Both of these goals are also quintessentially Marxist (and arguably British as well as American) and fit well with research practice as it developed in early cultural studies work; John Van Maanen, *Tales of the Field: On Writing Ethnography* (Chicago: University of Chicago Press, 1988), 18.

10 David Morley and Charlotte Brunsdon, *The Nationwide Television Studies* (London: Routledge, 1999) and David Morley, *Family Television: Cultural Power and Domestic Leisure* (London: Routledge, 1986).

11 Morley, *Family Television*, 51.

12 Morley's research has often been linked to the work of Janice Radway and Ien Ang, both of whom differ considerably from Morley in methodological approach but exhibit similarly limited contact time with their subjects. See Janice Radway, *Reading the Romance: Women, Patriarchy, and Popular Literature* (Chapel Hill, NC: University of North Carolina Press, 1984) and Ien Ang, *Watching Dallas: Soap Opera and the Melodramatic Imagination* (London: Methuen, 1985).

13 For two theoretical touchstones of work on the spectatorial gaze, see Laura Mulvey's seminal essay, "Visual Pleasure and Narrative Cinema," *Screen* 16, no. 3 (1975): 6–18, and Manthia Diawara, "Black Spectatorship: Problems of Identification and Resistance," *Screen* 29, no. 4 (1986): 66–76. For an overview of issues surrounding "the gaze," see Peter Wollen, "On Gaze Theory," *New Left Review* 44 (March/April 2007): 91–106.

14 David Morley, *Television, Audiences, and Cultural Studies* (London: Routledge, 1992), 180.

15 John Fiske challenges Morley's notion of a reading of readings: "this sort of ethnography cannot be an objective empirical science: it extends the interpretive analytical mode from texts to the people who read them and the meanings they make from them. It is thus an extension of semiotics and should perhaps be referred to by a name like 'ethno-semiotics.'" Fiske seems to be affirming Morley's conception of his work, while criticizing it along lines that the practitioners have never claimed for their own. As Geertz and Ricouer (amongst others) have shown, action in the daily world becomes text once an attempt is made to understand it. John Fiske, *Introduction to Communication Studies* (London: Routledge, 2010), 153.

16 David Morley, "Theoretical Orthodoxies: Textualism, Constructivism and the 'New Eth-

nography' in Cultural Studies" in *Cultural Studies in Question*, eds. Marjorie Ferguson and Peter Golding (London: Sage, 1997), 126.

17 Raymond Williams, *The Sociology of Culture* (Chicago: University of Chicago Press, 1981), 13.

18 As it does educational anthropologist Harry Wolcott's more prescriptive model. Harry F. Wolcott, "Ethnography? Or Educational Travel Writing?" in *Ethnography and Schools: Qualitative Approaches to the Study of Education*, eds. Yali Zou and Enrique (Henry) T. Trueba (Lanham, MD: Rowman & Littlefield, 2002). Wolcott's title for his article is interesting in light of Mary Louise Pratt's comparative analysis of the tropes of ethnography and travel writing in her essay, "Fieldwork in Common Places" in *Writing Culture: The Poetics and Politics of Ethnography*, eds. James Clifford and George E. Marcus (Berkeley: University of California Press, 1986), 27–50. Her ideas will be discussed in the context of the examination of the tropes of educational narratives and those of ethnography in chapter 2, but here I would simply suggest that the two forms of writing have more in common than anthropologists would wish to admit. And why not? A good descriptive piece of travel writing may illuminate aspects of a culture in ways that a conventional, dryly objective piece of anthropology may not.

19 Marie Gillespie, *Television, Ethnicity and Cultural Change* (London: Routledge, 1995).

20 Ibid., 1.

21 See, for example: Ariel Dorfman and Armand Mattelart, *How to Read Donald Duck* (New York: International General, 1971); Herbert I. Schiller, *Mass Communications and American Empire* (New York: Beacon, 1971); and Dallas W. Smythe, *Dependency Road: Communications, Capitalism, Consciousness, and Canada* (Norwood, NJ: Ablex, 1981). Mattelart has revised his position considerably since his work on media imperialism in the 1970s and early 1980s. See Armand Mattelart, *Networking the World, 1794–2000*, trans. Liz Carey-Libbrecht and James A. Cohen (Minneapolis: University of Minnesota Press, 2000) for an example of his more recent, more nuanced analysis of global networks and media.

22 Faye D. Ginsburg, Lila Abu-Lughod, and Brian Larkin, eds., *Media Worlds: Anthropology on New Terrain* (Berkeley: University of California Press, 2002), 2.

23 Arjun Appadurai, "Disjuncture and Difference in the Global Cultural Economy," in *Planet TV: A Global Television Reader*, eds. Lisa Parks and Shanti Kumar (New York: New York University Press, 2003), 40–52.

24 For recent work on media history in the "era" of transmedia and technological convergence, see, Janet Staiger and Sabine Hake, eds., *Convergence Media History* (New York: Routledge, 2009).

25 Others are Georges Bataille, *Visions of Excess: Selected Writings, 1927–1939* (Minneapolis: University of Minnesota Press, 1985); Roger Caillois, *The Edge of Surrealism: A Roger Caillois Reader*, ed. Claudine Frank (Durham, NC: Duke University Press, 2003); Eric Michaels, *For a Cultural Future: Francis Jupurrurla Makes TV at Yuendumu* (Melbourne, Australia: Artspace, 1987); and James Clifford, *The Predicament of Culture: Twentieth-Century Ethnography, Literature, and Art* (Cambridge, MA: Harvard University Press, 1988).

26 For more on these films and others, see Jean Rouch, *Cine-Ethnography* (Minneapolis: University of Minnesota, 2003) and Paul Stoller, *The Cinematic Griot: The Ethnography of Jean Rouch* (University of Chicago Press, 1992).

27 Marc Augé, *In the Metro*, trans. Tom Conley (Minneapolis: University of Minnesota Press, 2002), 59–60.

Chapter 1

1 Annette Kuhn, *Family Secrets: Acts of Imagination and Memory* (London: Verso, 2002), 33.

2 Evan Hunter wrote the original book upon which the screenplay for *Blackboard Jungle* was based. He later wrote the screenplay for Alfred Hitchcock's *The Birds* and, under the pen name Ed McBain, the series of popular novels describing the exploits of police officers in the 87th precinct in New York City.

3 Hayden White, *Metahistory: The Historical Imagination in Nineteenth-Century Europe* (Baltimore: John Hopkins University, 1973), 30–31. Other versions of this prescription for constructing the research object appear in Pierre Bourdieu and Loïc J. D. Wacquant, *An Invitation to Reflexive Sociology* (Chicago: University of Chicago, 1992), and John Van Maanen, *Tales of the Field: On Writing Ethnography* (Chicago: University of Chicago Press, 1988).

4 Sources in ethnographic research include but are not limited to: participant observation, interviews, and textual/visual documentation.

5 Examples of this discourse on juvenile delinquency abound, from the specifics of Frederic Wertham's *Seduction of the Innocent* in the 1950s to the generalized explanations on the nightly news as to the causal factors for the Columbine shootings in the 1990s. In all of the discourses involving teens and delinquency there is a logic that follows the narrative conventions of fictionalized accounts of teachers: the group of out-of-control teen thugs led by an intelligent but abusive leader, a few "good" teens who become victims of the thugs, and the teachers who attempt to help the hellions (some of whom fail and are also claimed as victims, while others succeed and are anointed as heroes). See Frederic Wertham, "Seduction of the Innocent," in *The Audience Studies Reader*, eds. Will Brooker and Deborah Jermyn (London: Routledge, 2003), 61–66; and Frederic Wertham, "Such Trivia as Comic Books," in *The Children's Culture Reader*, ed. Henry Jenkins (New York: New York University Press, 1998), 486–92.

6 It should be noted that in sharp contrast to *Blackboard Jungle*, a film from the 1950s that was blamed by the press for inciting riots among youth, the 1970s television program *Happy Days* used "Rock Around the Clock" to evoke the good old days of high school fun—the nostalgic past of the 1950s. For more on the "media panics" surrounding *Blackboard Jungle* (and media panics in general), see Grace Palladino, *Teenagers: An American History* (New York: Basic, 1996), 160, and Bill Osgerby, *Youth Media* (London: Routledge, 2004), 72.

7 For a discussion of "tales" in anthropology and sociology, see Van Maanen, *Tales*, 1–12.

8 Bronislaw Malinowski, *A Diary in the Strict Sense of the Term*, trans. Norbert Guterman (Stanford, CA: Stanford University Press, 1989). Malinowski's diary is also discussed in Clifford Geertz, *Works and Lives: The Anthropologist as Author* (Stanford, CA: Stanford University Press, 1988).

9 Van Maanen, *Tales*, 102.

10 This underlying motivation for Mark Thackeray's approach to pedagogy—transforming the options available to his working class students—resembles the general conclusion arrived at by Paul Willis and other theorists of social reproduction, Paul Willis, *Learning to Labor: How Working Class Kids Get Working Class Jobs* (New York: Columbia University Press, 1977): "Structures which have now become sources of meaning, definition and identity provide the framework and basis for decisions and choices in life—in our liberal democracy taken 'freely'—which taken systematically and in the aggregate over large numbers actually helps to reproduce the main structures and functions of society" (174).

11. Caryl Phillips, "To Ricky with Love," *The Guardian Review*, July 23, 2005, 28–29.

12 The plot involves Garfield's attempts to come to terms with his fears regarding his current students and the memories of his student attacker, as well as a parallel plot concerning the systematic torture and execution of some of his worst gang member students. The film's concluding scene mirrors the final scene from *The Deerhunter* as Garfield and his student-antagonists play Russian roulette.

13 While other films may fit a standard generic definition of the teacher-protagonist film, the above discussion has focused on those films that exhibit patterns parallel to those found in modes of ethnographic practice that foreground the researcher's subjectivity. Each of the films discussed sketch out variations on the arrival scene as set by *Blackboard Jungle* (variations modulated by each film's specific historical moment and cultural intent). Other films could have been included, but films such as *Goodbye Mr. Chips* (1939), *Up the Down Staircase* (1967), *The Paper Chase* (1973), *Teachers* (1984), and *Dead Poet's Society* (1989) fail to exhibit crucial aspects of the basic pattern (a form of typology linked to the notion of genre, but not coinci-

dent with it)—teachers play supporting characters, students are older or younger than those in high school, or the school featured is not a public institution. Thus, for our discussion, *Blackboard Jungle* stands as the typological model for the intersecting narrative structures of ethnography and education.

14 Mary Louise Pratt, "Fieldwork in Common Places," in *Writing Culture: The Poetics and Politics of Ethnography*, eds. James Clifford and George E. Marcus (Berkeley: University of California Press, 1986), 31–32.

15 The relationship between ethnographic films and written ethnographies that foreground the tropes of otherness and authenticity constitutes a research project parallel to, yet distinct from, that which I am developing in this chapter. For work that examines alternative approaches to ethnographic film practice, see Catherine Russell, *Experimental Ethnography: The Work of Film in the Age of Video* (Durham, NC: Duke University Press, 1999), and Trinh T. Minh-ha, *Framer Framed* (New York: Routledge, 1992).

16 Pratt, "Fieldwork," quotes Bronislaw Malinowski's description of his arrival in the *Argonauts of the Western Pacific* (New York: Dutton, 1961): "Imagine yourself suddenly set down surrounded by your gear, alone on a tropical beach close to a native village while the launch or dinghy which has brought you sails away out of sight" (4). Dadier, Thackeray, and Escalante arrive by motorized transportation and are in the city, but each in his arrival at his respective school is depicted as nearly as isolated as Malinowski seems to be. Of course, Pat Conroy arrives at his school on an actual dinghy.

17 Paul Rabinow, *Reflections on Fieldwork in Morocco* (Berkeley: University of California Press, 1977), 11.

18 Peter McLaren, *Schooling as a Ritual Performance: Toward a Political Economy of Educational Symbols and Gestures* (Lanham, MD: Rowman & Littlefield, 1999), 64.

19 Ibid., 65.

20 Many anthropologists have identified this problem of elevating their own status within supposedly disinterested ethnographic narratives. For instance, Ruth Behar recalls her initial thoughts regarding her fieldwork with a peasant woman from Mexico, Behar, *Translated Woman: Crossing the Border with Esperanza's Story*, 10th Anniversary ed. (Boston: Beacon, 2003): "Here was a woman [Esperanza] who, unlike the subjects of my readings, I could follow home, talk to, confront, not have to piece together from the fragments of a court transcript. Excited, the anthropologist who had been hiding under the historian's skin boldly stepped forward and stared into the eyes of the living woman, met the challenge of her presence, here now…. That's how I would tell the story if I wanted to cast myself in the part of the anthropologist as heroine" (3). She goes on to tell the story in a much more fragmented way that foregrounds both her telling of the tale and the strong voice of Esperanza.

21 Peter Sipe, "Newjack: Teaching in a Failing Middle School," *Harvard Educational Review* 74, no. 3 (2004): 333.

22 John H. Weakland, "Feature Films as Cultural Documents" in *Principles of Visual Anthropology*, ed. Paul Hockings (Berlin, Germany: Mouton de Gruyter, 2003), 60.

23 Pierre Bourdieu, *The Field of Cultural Production: Essays on Art and Literature* (New York: Columbia University Press, 1993), 61–73.

24 Elenore Smith Bowen, *Return to Laughter: An Anthropological Novel* (Garden City, NY: Anchor, 1954), 50.

25 Pratt, "Fieldwork," 31.

26 Recently there have been a scatter of works that focus on the history of film studies as a pedagogical institution and the use of film within educational contexts. See Dana Polan, *Scenes of Instruction: The Beginnings of the U.S. Study of Film* (Berkeley: University of California Press, 2007); Lee Grieveson and Haidee Wasson, eds., *Inventing Film Studies* (Durham, NC: Duke University Press, 2008); and Devon Orgeron, Marsha Orgeron, and Dan Streible, eds., *Learning with the Lights Off: Educational Film in the United States* (New York: Oxford University Press, 2012).

27 An exception to this exclusion has been the work of educational historian Larry Cuban in his

book *Teachers and Machines: The Classroom Use of Technology since 1920* (New York: Teachers College Press, 1986).

28 Examples could also easily be drawn from other media such as the television series *Our Miss Brooks* (1952–56), *Room 222* (1969–74), and, more recently, *Boston Public* (2000–2004).

29 Frank N. Freeman, ed., *Visual Education: A Comparative Study of Motion Pictures and Other Methods of Instruction* (Chicago: University of Chicago Press, 1924), and Richard A. Maynard, *The Celluloid Curriculum: How to Use Movies in the Classroom* (Rochelle Park, NJ: Hayden, 1971).

30 For discussions of "best practices" in media education, see Len Masterman, *Teaching the Media* (London: Routledge, 1985); David Buckingham, *Media Education: Literacy, Learning and Contemporary Culture* (London: Blackwell, 2003); Steve Goodman, *Teaching Youth Media: A Critical Guide to Literacy, Video Production, and Social Change* (New York: Teachers College Press, 2003); Tanya Joosten, *Social Media for Educators: Strategies and Best Practices* (San Francisco: Jossey-Bass, 2012); and www.edutopia.org.

31 Most often the term *media education* is used to identify curriculum from the United Kingdom while the term *media literacy* is used in the U.S. educational context.

32 See, for example, Gunther Kress, *Literacy in the New Media Age* (London: Routledge, 2003); Robert Kubey, ed., *Media Literacy in the Information Age: Current Perspectives* (New Brunswick, NJ: Transaction, 2001); as well as Jenkins, *Convergence Culture*. In 2009, MIT Press launched the online publication *International Journal of Learning and Media*, edited by David Buckingham, Tara McPherson, and Ellen Seiter, which covers issues in education focusing on media literacy and participatory culture .

33 See Bill Cope and Mary Kalantzis, eds., *Multiliteracies* (London: Routledge, 2000); James Paul Gee, *What Video Games Have to Teach Us About Learning and Literacy* (New York: Palgrave Macmillan, 2003); and Ilana Snyder, ed., *Silicon Literacies: Communication, Innovation and Education in the Electronic Age* (London: Routledge, 2002).

34 See Stefanie Olsen, "Educational Video Games Mix Cool with Purpose," *The New York Times*, November 1, 2009, http://www.nytimes.com/2009/11/02/technology/02games.html.

35 Henry A. Giroux, *Breaking into the Movies: Film and the Culture of Politics* (London: Blackwell, 2002), and Henry A. Giroux, Colin Lankshear, Peter McLaren, and Michael Peters, eds., *Counternarratives: Cultural Studies and Critical Pedagogies in Postmodern Spaces* (New York: Routledge, 1996). Also see Jenkins, *Convergence Culture* for a more recent discussion of this topic.

36 Bowen, *Return to Laughter*, 74.

37 I consider the teacher–student interaction within the context of media pedagogy, and my own media-based teaching, more fully in chapter 4. A key text to understanding this interaction beyond those already mentioned—Giroux, *Breaking*, McLaren, *Schooling*, Behar, *Translated Woman*—is Lisa Delpit's *Other People's Children: Cultural Conflict in the Classroom* (New York: New Press, 1996).

38 In effect reversing the polarities of the "literary turn" in anthropology as initiated by Clifford Geertz in essays such as his "Blurred Genres: The Refiguration of Social Thought," in *Local Knowledge: Further Essays in Interpretive Anthropology* (New York: Basic, 1983), and by the authors collected in James Clifford and George E. Marcus, eds., *Writing Culture: The Poetics and Politics of Ethnography* (Berkeley: University of California Press, 1986).

Chapter 2

1 Basil B. Bernstein, *Pedagogy, Symbolic Control, and Identity: Theory, Research, Critique*, revised ed.(Lanham, MD: Rowman & Littlefield, 2000), 3.

2 Though with the highly politicized public debate around the control of schooling, Mr. Austin's seemingly obvious use of a science film on childbirth in a biology class may be met with criticism and attempts by the concerned public to undermine his increasingly limited aca-

demic freedom. Signed permission slips would most likely be needed so as to avoid liability on the part of the school for showing "inappropriate" images to students.

3 HyperCard was a multimedia software program developed by Apple Computer in the late 1980s. HyperCard used the metaphor of a stack of 3" by 5" index cards to organize text, image, and sound into a playable database similar to a slide show presentation in the currently popular PowerPoint program by Microsoft.

4 The source code for MacPaint was donated by Apple on July 20, 2010 to the Computer History Museum located in Mountain View, CA. See www.computerhistory.org/highlights/macpaint/.

5 "Whiteboards" have for the most part replaced traditional blackboards because chalk dust causes damage to human breathing and to the computer hardware now installed in many classrooms. The dry erase markers that are used with whiteboards give off a pungent chemical odor that surely competes with old fashioned chalk dust for choking the lungs of both students and teachers.

6 These vignettes are derived from my own experience as a participant in American public education supplemented by material garnered from works on the historical setting of teaching. My student experience comes from primary and secondary schools in the Portland Public School District from 1965 through 1977 and my teaching experience ranges from auxiliary programs in Portland to special education and vocational education in California dating from 1982 until 2000. For more on the use of memories as the basis for research see, Annette Kuhn, *Family Secrets: Acts of Memory and Imagination*, rev. ed. (London: Verso, 2002); Carolyn Kay Steedman, *Landscape for a Good Woman: A Story of Two Lives* (New Brunswick, NJ: Rutgers University Press, 1986); and Susannah Radstone, ed., *Memory and Methodology* (Oxford, UK: Berg, 2000). For the history of American public education, see, Larry Cuban, *How Teachers Taught: Constancy and Change in American Classroom 1880–1990* (New York: Teachers College Press, 1993); Sarah Mondale and Sarah B. Patton, eds., *School: The Story of American Public Education* (Boston: Beacon, 2001); Diane Ravitch, *Left Back: A Century of Battles over School Reform* (New York: Simon & Shuster, 2000); and David Tyack and Larry Cuban, *Tinkering toward Utopia: A Century of Public School Reform* (Cambridge, MA: Harvard University Press, 1996).

7 Marshall McLuhan, *Understanding Media: The Extensions of Man* (Cambridge, MA: MIT Press, 1994), 9.

8 Ibid., 8.

9 Jay David Bolter and Richard Grusin, *Remediation: Understanding New Media* (Cambridge, MA: MIT Press, 1999), 45.

10 Larry Cuban, *Teachers and Machines: The Classroom Use of Technology Since 1920* (New York: Teacher's College Press, 1985), 57–58.

11 Ibid., 58.

12 See his historical survey of teaching methods, Cuban, *How Teachers Taught*.

13 Obviously, the overhead projector serves all of the functions of the blackboard without being "durable" in the sense that the blackboard is always ready as a teaching tool and not subject to bulb burnouts, scratched glass, and broken switches. Some of the problems that arise with 16mm films and television monitors arise with the overhead projector, but the differentiation sharpens as we progress to image projection and the conditions of electronic and digital screening.

14 Here I want to acknowledge the ongoing debate within television studies over the notion of "liveness" as an essential element of the medium specificity of television. Whether or not liveness is formally essential, it is nevertheless the aspect that many teachers remark on as that which distinguishes television as a medium within instructional settings.

15 For more on the "voice" in documentary see Bill Nichols, *Representing Reality: Issues and Concepts in Documentary* (Bloomington: Indiana University Press, 1991) and *Introduction to Documentary* (Bloomington: Indiana University, 2010).

16 For more on ETV and its history in American public education, see James Zigerell, *The*

Uses of Television in American Higher Education (New York: Praeger, 1991); Brian Goldfarb, *Visual Pedagogy: Media Cultures in and beyond the Classroom* (Durham, NC: Duke University Press, 2002); Allen E. Koenig and Ruane B. Hill, eds., *The Farther Vision: Educational Television Today* (Madison: University of Wisconsin Press, 1967); and U.S. Department of Health, Education, and Welfare, *Educational Television: The Next Ten Years* (Stanford, CA: Institute for Communication Research, Stanford University, 1962).

17 There have been initiatives beginning in the late 2000s planned to incorporate mobile and tablet technologies at the secondary and higher education levels. See, for example, the attempts to get the Amazon Kindle and the Apple iPad adopted by colleges and universities: Mirela Iverac, "The Kindle Goes to College," *Forbes*, entry posted August 26, 2009, http://www.forbes.com/2009/08/26/amazon-kindle-colleges-leadership-dx.html   and Chris Foresman, "iPad Goes Under the Gauntlet at Universities This Fall," *Ars Technica*, entry posted July 21, 2010, http://arstechnica.com/apple/news/2010/07/ipad-goes-under-the-gauntlet-at-universities-this-fall.ars.

18 J. Laplanche and J.-B. Pontalis, *The Language of Psychoanalysis*, trans. Donald Nicholson-Smith (New York: Norton, 1973), 460.

19 Anthony Elliott, *Psychoanalytic Theory: An Introduction*, 2nd ed. (Durham, NC: Duke University Press, 2002), 17.

20 Of course, the use of transference as a metaphor for the relationship between student and teacher, lifted as it is from its therapeutic context, fails as an exact concurrence between transference as applied to the psychoanalytic session and to the pedagogic encounter, but it does provide an explanatory model by which to begin to make faltering steps toward understanding the complexity of the pull that the beloved teacher has on a student. For an example of the beloved teacher narrative (explored critically to some extent) see: Mark Edmundson, *Teacher: The One Who Made the Difference* (New York: Vintage, 2003).

21 See for instance, David E. Nye, *American Technological Sublime* (Cambridge, MA: MIT Press, 1994) and Leo Marx, *The Machine in the Garden: Technology and the Pastoral Ideal in America* (New York: Oxford University Press, 1964).

22 Of course, the concept of the teaching machine can easily refract evocations of the myriad other machines that haunt not just education but our culture overall. Some examples are: the cyborg machines of popular genre fiction; the desiring machines of Gilles Deleuze and Félix Guattari in their book *Anti-Oedipus: Capitalism and Schizophrenia* (New York: Penguin, 2009); the machine learning of classic Artificial Intelligence research; the bureaucratic machine as the Kafkaesque institution of education; and finally, the machine as a concept which figures in recent works of critical theory such as John Johnston, *The Allure of Machinic Life: Cybernetics, Artificial Life and the New AI* (MIT Press, 2008) and Gerald Raunig, *The Thousand Machines: A Concise History of the Machine as Social Movement* (New York: Semiotext(e); Cambridge, MA: MIT Press, 2010).

23 B. F. Skinner, *The Technology of Teaching* (Englewood Cliffs, NJ: Prentice-Hall, 1968), 37.

24 Although melodramatic in its depiction, Thea Von Harbou, in her novelization of her script for *Metropolis*, describes robot-Maria's entrance in a manner that viscerally portrays the alienation assumed in human–machine interaction by liberal critics of automation: "But at the same moment the being [robot-Maria] lost its balance. It fell, tipping forward, towards Jon Fredersen. He stretched out his hands to catch it, feeling them, in the moment of contact, to be burnt by an unbearable coldness, the brutality of which brought up in him a feeling of anger and disgust." Thea von Harbou, *Metropolis*, 1927, Internet Archive, http://www.archive.org/details/ Metropolis_63.

25 Skinner, *Technology of Teaching*, 23–24. While Skinner is rightly seen as an evangelist of sorts for programmed instruction in its grimmer incarnations, it is significant that he notes: "Will machines replace teachers? On the contrary, they are capital equipment to be used by teachers to save time and labor. In assigning certain mechanizable functions to machines, the teacher emerges in his [sic] proper role as an indispensable human being. He may teach more students than heretofore…but he will do so in fewer hours and with fewer burdensome chores" (55).

This is of course significantly similar to the arguments being made in the current moment of postbubble digital technology implementation in K-12 and higher education.

26 A brief sketch of popular cultural associations of the machine and the human can be seen in the recent news coverage of IBM's Watson AI system (a follow-up to the AI program Deep Blue which beat chess champion Gary Kasparov in May 1997). Watson played successful contestants from the television game show Jeopardy—winning handily. Discussion of Watson's victory was featured on a PBS *Newshour* segment which intercut talking head interviews with computer scientists and futurists with screens of green digital lettering reminiscent of *The Matrix* and clips from *Metropolis*, *Forbidden Planet*, and *2001: A Space Odyssey*. This type of segment exemplifies the popular, yet in this case more sophisticated coverage which attends to human–machine interaction. See PBS *Newshour*, "A: This Computer Could Defeat You at 'Jeopardy!' Q: What Is Watson?" aired February 14, 2011.

27 Basil B. Bernstein, *Pedagogy, Symbolic Control, and Identity*, 3.

28 George Lakoff and Mark Johnson, *Metaphors We Live By* (Chicago: University of Chicago Press, 2003).

29 John Dewey, *Democracy and Education: An Introduction to the Philosophy of Education* (New York: Free Press, 1916), 5.

30 While it should be unnecessary at this juncture to defend the work of 1970s film theory as a method for thinking through the media, it seems prudent to point at the area of convergence that exists between seemingly radical notions drawn from auteur-structuralism and the more conventionalized notions of distributed agency that have been generated within cognitive science (an explicit politics has been denied by most of the proponents of the latter).

31 See for example, Don Ross, David Spurrett, Harold Kincaid, and G. Lynn Stephens, eds., *Distributed Cognition and the Will: Individual Volition and Social Context* (Cambridge, MA: MIT Press, 2007).

32 Michel Foucault, "What is an Author?" in *Aesthetics, Method, and Epistemology*, ed. James D. Faubion (New York: New Press, 1998). For Roland Barthes's contribution to this conception of authorship, see "The Death of the Author," in *Image, Music, Text*, ed. Stephen Heath (New York: Hill & Wang, 1977).

33 A generalized reading of Foucault's essay applied to the educational field suggests that a range of practices and discourses involving a variety of media can operate as pedagogy per se. By way of analogy, texts are produced by the author function; instruction is produced by the pedagogical agent as a specific form of the author function.

34 Peter Wollen, *Signs and Meaning in the Cinema* (London: Secker & Warburg/BFI, 1972).

35 See Andrew Sarris, "Notes on the Auteur Theory in 1962," in *Film Theory and Criticism*, eds. Leo Braudy and Marshall Cohen (New York: Oxford University Press, 2004) and *The American Cinema: Directors and Directions, 1929–1968* (New York: Da Capo, 1996). Also see Pauline Kael, "Circles and Squares," *Film Quarterly* 16, no. 3 (Spring, 1963): 12–26, and Andrew Sarris, "The Auteur Theory and the Perils of Pauline," *Film Quarterly* 16, no. 4 (Summer, 1963): 26–33, for the debate that defines a more populist form of criticism regarding the American version of auteur theory.

36 Pierre Bourdieu, *The Field of Cultural Production: Essays on Art and Literature* (New York: Columbia University Press, 1993), 53.

37 See David Noble, "Digital Diploma Mills, Part 1: The Automation of Higher Education," *October* 86 (1998): 107–117, and "Digital Diploma Mills, Part 2: The Coming Battle over Online Instruction," *October* 86 (1998): 118–129 for an early, yet prescient, discussion of the changes in ownership of curriculum and instruction on the part of university professors as they face the increasing industrial digitalization of the academy.

38 See Bourdieu and Wacquant, *An Invitation to Reflexive Sociology*, 16.

39 Incidentally, *Stand and Deliver* was used to teach methods of student-centered instruction at the school of education at which I earned my California teaching credential. Their credential program was quite progressive and included a course on the effects of technology on curriculum and instruction, so Jaime Escalante's filmic pedagogy was in line with the overall goals

of the program. We also spent a weekend examining Leni Riefensthal's *Triumph of the Will* (1935) as a form of instruction through propaganda. The professor of the course, who at the time chaired the program, was himself an outstanding and innovative teacher.

40 Zigerell, *The Uses of Television*, 28–29.

41 Donna Haraway, "A Manifesto for Cyborgs: Science, Technology, and Socialist-Feminism in the Late Twentieth Century" in *The Haraway Reader* (New York: Routledge, 2003).

42 Howard Gardner, *The Unschooled Mind: How Children Think and How Schools Should Teach* (New York: Basic, 1991), 109.

43 James Paul Gee, *What Video Games Have to Teach Us about Learning and Literacy*, rev. ed. (New York: Palgrave Macmillan, 2007), 187.

44 Jean Lave and Etienne Wenger, *Situated Learning: Legitimate Peripheral Participation* (Cambridge, UK: Cambridge University Press, 1991), 50–51.

45 Which is evocative of the banking model of pedagogy as described by educational activist Paolo Freire in which authoritative professors deposit knowledge into the brains of passive and submissive students. See Paolo Freire, *Pedagogy of the Oppressed* (1970; New York: Continuum, 1998), 55–58.

46 For suggestive surveys of this kind of work, see Noah Wardrip-Fruin, *Expressive Processing: Digital Fictions, Computer Games, and Software Studies* (Cambridge, MA: MIT Press, 2009) and Ian Bogost, *Persuasive Games: The Expressive Power of Videogames* (Cambridge, MA: MIT Press, 2007).

Chapter 3

1 Umberto Eco, "Can Television Teach?" in *The Screen Education Reader: Cinema, Television, Culture*, eds. Manuel Alvarado, Edward Buscombe, and Richard Collins (New York: Columbia University Press, 1993), 96.

2 All of the comments from Professor Capretz used in this chapter are culled from interviews conducted during a visit that I made to the Yale campus during January 2004.

3 John Witherspoon, Roselle Kovitz, Robert K. Avery, and Alan G. Stavitsky, *A History of Public Broadcasting* (Washington, DC: Current Publishing Committee, 2000).

4 For a study in depth that considers the use of entertainment for educational purposes (focusing on telenovelas and such), see Arvind Singhal and Everett Rogers, *Entertainment-Education: A Communication Strategy for Social Change* (Mahwah, NJ: Erlbaum, 1999).

5 A reply of sorts to Sir Kenneth Clark's program.

6 Bill Nichols, "The Voice of Documentary," in *Film Quarterly: Forty Years—A Selection* (Berkeley: University of California Press, 1999), 246–257.

7 James Zigerell, *The Uses of Television in American Higher Education* (New York: Praeger, 1991), 32.

8 Jonathan Conlin, *Civilization* (London: BFI, 2009).

9 All of these materials—textbook: Pierre J. Capretz, Béatrice Abetti, and Marie-Odile Germain, *French in Action: A Beginning Course in Language and Culture*, 2nd ed., *The Capretz Method*, Part 1 (New Haven, CT: Yale University Press, 1997); workbook: Pierre J. Capretz, Béatrice Abetti, Thomas Abbate, and Frank Abetti, *French in Action: A Beginning Course in Language and Culture*, 2nd ed., *The Capretz Method, Workbook,* Part 1 (New Haven, CT: Yale University Press, 1994); and study guide: Barry Lydgate, Sylvie Mathé, Norman Susskind, John Westlie, and Laurence Wylie, *French in Action: A Beginning Course in Language and Culture*, 2nd ed., *The Capretz Method, Study Guide*, Part 1 (New Haven, CT: Yale University Press, 1994)—are available through either the Yale University Press or the Corporation for Public Broadcasting's Annenberg Learner website, both of which coproduced materials for *French in Action*. The printed study materials are meant to be integral parts of the *French in Action* instructional program.

10 Ellen Bialystock and Kenji Hakuta, *In Other Words: The Science and Psychology of Second-Language Acquisition* (New York: Basic, 1994).

11 Rick Altman, *The Video Connection: Integrating Video into Language Teaching* (Boston: Houghton Mifflin, 1989), 42.
12 A shot-reverse shot sequence is a standard film and television editing technique in which the viewer is first shown the face of one character speaking or looking at another off-screen character at which point the shot "reverses," featuring the face of the character to whom the first character was speaking. During extended scenes featuring character dialogue some directors merely ping-pong back and forth between close-ups as each character has his or her say. More artful directors, Alfred Hitchcock for example, often feature shot-reverse shot sequences in which the close-up of the face is on the character who is listening and not the one who is speaking. This lingering on the reaction possibly provides greater nuance in narrative development as the inner thoughts of characters can be revealed through a confluence of dialogue and facial expression—in line with the standard advice to novice actors, to "really listen" to their fellow actors as they perform.
13 Capretz stated that the failure of these speak-out moments was one of the motivations for his attempt to update *French in Action* as *French in Interaction*, a web and interactive DVD version of the original program. He was busily developing this updated version during my 2004 visit to Yale, but the program has yet to materialize as a public, commercially available product.
14 These rapid-fire characterizations—stereotypes in the broadest sense of the term—serve a useful purpose in many instances as they imply a recognizable biography for each character while foregoing the work, and screen time, necessary to provide a more fully realized back story for each actor that appears on screen. But as telegraphic characterization reduces a complex set of human interactions down to a routine set of expectations on the part of the viewer, narrative dilemmas occur—representational reductionism as such.
15 Jostein Gripsrud, "Scholars, Journalism, Television: Notes on Some Conditions for Mediation and Intervention," in *Television and Common Knowledge*, ed. Jostein Gripsrud (London: Routledge, 1999), 47.
16 Ibid., 47.
17 In the early 1990s, a group of students at Yale complained to the administration that *French in Action* created a sexist and hostile environment for women learning French at the university. The complaint centered on Mireille's response to an annoying Parisian "ladies' man" as he tries to pick up women at the Luxembourg garden and the Sorbonne in the narrative arc of lessons 11 through 13. As with other characters featured in the program, Jean-Pierre, the "horrible dragueur," is a broadly drawn stereotype and is actually rebuffed by several female characters within the narrative (as well as a man standing on line at the school). Carolyn Durham explores the controversy and makes a case for *French in Action* as a feminist (in explicit contradiction to the complainants in the Yale report) and postmodern text in her book on American receptions of French cinema. See Carolyn A. Durham, "At the Franco-American Crossroads of Gender and Culture: Where Feminism and Sexism Intersect," in *Double Takes: Culture and Gender in French Films and Their American Remakes* (Hanover, NH: University Press of New England, 1998), 91–113.
18 Bourdieu, *Distinction*, 23.
19 John Urry, *The Tourist Gaze* (London: Sage, 2001), 12–13.
20 Cineastes are also a form of tourist in as much as they travel to distant lands by virtue of the cinematic frame/window. Here is the point at which discourses of tourism overlap with those of cyberculture. Paul Virilio emphasizes the immobility of the body while traveling in the Concord jet—in which distance is actually traversed—as being mirrored by the immobility of the body while surfing the Internet—in which distance is collapsed through the virtual. See Paul Virilio, *The Information Bomb*, trans. Chris Turner (London: Verso, 2000) and Anne Friedberg, "Virilio's Screen: The Work of Metaphor in the Age of Technological Convergence," *Journal of Visual Culture* 3, no. 2 (2004), 183–93.
21 Dean MacCannell, *The Tourist: A New Theory of the Leisure Class* (Berkeley: University of California Press, 1999), 10.
22 Peter Hamilton, "Representing the Social: France and Frenchness in Post-war Humanist

Photography," in *Representation: Cultural Representations and Signifying Practices*, ed. Stuart Hall (London: Sage, 1997), 146.

23 In fact, in the final episode of *French in Action* Mireille is surprised to discover that the mysterious man who has been following her around Paris is actually a casting agent for a film. She may become a celebrity after all!

24 These narratives of ethnographic observation were collected during the aforementioned visit to Yale during January 2004.

25 For my research, the fact that I am not fluent in French is of little importance. What this chapter, the entire book for that matter, emphasizes is the visual, gestural, and spatial aspects of the instructional methods used in each of the modes of pedagogical agency. While this approach does bracket off some aspects of what transpired in the classrooms I visited, the efficacy of many of the techniques used in *French in Action* were rendered more salient as I moved through the program as a student of instruction. Another methodology could have focused on the linguistic aspects of the program with differing interpretative results. Nevertheless, in the classrooms at Yale, the pedagogical interactions between students and teacher gained a form of semiotic transparency through attention on my part to bodies coupled with language (as intonation and expression), that allowed for a reading unclouded by the specifics of linguistic intent. Examples of this research strategy can be found in texts by Roland Barthes, on his travels through Japan (again, as a tourist), and Harold Garfinkel, on his observation and analysis of an undergraduate chemistry class. See Roland Barthes, *Empire of Signs*, trans. Richard Howard (New York: Hill & Wang, 1982) and, more importantly, Harold Garfinkel, "A Study of the Work of Teaching Undergraduate Chemistry," in *Ethnomethodology's Program: Working out Durkheim's Aphorism*, ed. Anne Warfield Rawls (Lanham, MD: Rowman & Littlefield, 2002).

Chapter 4

1 Marc Augé, *Non-places: Introduction to an Anthropology of Supermodernity* (London: Verso, 1995), 39.

2 This term, *the digital divide*, was bandied about in the news as a crisis during the early 1990s. The panic mode that it engendered fits into a larger history of generalized panics regarding children and the media. Each new technology is seen as fostering inequalities—cell phones, television, films (in early parts of the twentieth century)—and is also conceived of as the solution to these same problems. Policy makers in education see the introduction of new technologies into schools as fixes, some might say "quick-fixes," for socially structured inequalities. This also opens up schools to additional forms of exploitation from businesses and corporations which can be seen in recent calls to include Kindle e-readers and Apple's iPads into college and university curriculums. There seems to be little organized innovative thinking regarding the use of these new technologies, simply a bandwagon mentality coupled with actual social and cultural inadequacies on the part of educational institutions. See Kelly Truong, "More Universities Announce iPad Experiments," *Chronicle of Higher Education*, July 20, 2010, http://chronicle.com/blogPost/More-Universities-Announce/25646/?sid=wc&utm_source=wc&utm_medium=en

3 Originally, the school bulletin was read over the loudspeaker by the assistant principal in charge of student activities. A large bear of a man, with an infectious voice and sense of humor, he was, as is said, a hard act to follow. Student hosts on *Trauber TV* never matched his authoritative or amusing style of delivery.

4 I decided early on that *Trauber TV* should be two things—a daily performance art event (featuring school news and information as the spoken text while incorporating art and music from a broad range of ethnic and cultural backgrounds) and a showcase for student-produced media (including work in video, audio, and graphics). I expressed my strong belief that the students needed to have control of the program to the principal and, to his credit, he agreed.

5 The length of the daily bulletin prior to *Trauber TV* had been three minutes, but an additional

two minutes were added so that students could air program segments of longer duration. This was approved, because the broadcast was a high priority for the district superintendent, but it required a contract modification to extend the length of the school day. This extension initially upset both teachers and students alike (apparently no one wanted to spend two more minutes at school). I mention this only to emphasize the regimentation that exists within the school environment and to point out that it can be an impediment to creative responses to the needs of teaching (while acknowledging, as a former teacher, the sanctity of class time used for instruction). On most days the additional two minutes were filled with student-produced "feature" segments, assembly recaps, or sports highlights (these were very popular with students and faculty), and the change in the school day bell schedule was eventually forgotten.

6 A major concern for teachers at the school was the lack of personalization for students. There seemed to be a consensus amongst teachers that many of the problems at Trauber High—poor attendance and grades, gang activity, and low morale—were attributable to the school's size, 4,200 students, and 200 faculty. It was impossible for teachers and administrators to get to know more than a small portion of the student population.

7 Hip-hop and rap were considered "challenging" to teachers, jazz and pre-sixties pop to students, and world music seemingly to all.

8 A problem from day one—we never knew enough flag etiquette, even after extensive research into the topic, to satisfy several members of our faculty who were exceptionally, and dogmatically, patriotic.

9 Len Masterman, *Teaching the Media* (London: Routledge, 1985), 33.

10 My approach to student production and to my role in the process was strongly influenced by my reading of Eric Michaels's book, *For a Cultural Future: Francis Jupurrurla Makes TV at Yuendumu* (Melbourne, Australia: Artspace, 1987). A friend had passed a copy on to me following her trip to New York saying something like, "this seems like the kind of thing you'd like. It's sort of video art meets education."

11 Faye D. Ginsburg, "Mediating Culture: Indigenous Media, Ethnographic Film, and the Production of Identity," in *Fields of Vision: Essays in Film Studies, Visual Anthropology, and Photography*, eds. Leslie Devereaux and Roger Hillman (Berkeley: University of California Press, 1995), 257–58.

12 An exemplary project, with a broader mandate and a much larger audience than *Trauber TV*, which remains committed to issues of youth culture and professional media practice is Youth Radio based in Oakland, CA. See Elizabeth Soep and Vivian Chavez, *Drop that Knowledge: Youth Radio Stories* (Berkeley: University of California Press, 2010) and their website http://www.youthradio.org for more on the innovative approaches to media literacy and production that Youth Radio employs in creating on-air radio spots which figure prominently on many NPR stations across the United States.

13 Ginsburg, "Mediating Culture," 260.

14 For examples of this type of identity construction by teens in relation to music, see Dick Hebdige, *Subculture: The Meaning of Style* (London: Routledge, 1979).

15 For a different take on the creation of self-identities, see Michel Foucault, "Self Writing," in *Ethics: Subjectivity and Truth*, ed. Paul Rabinow (New York: New Press, 1997), 207–22.

16 This chapter specifically refers to students aged fifteen to seventeen. I make no claims regarding younger students or those teens who experience life through a set of cultural formations different from those that hold for school in the United States. In addition, it is important to note that much of the work represented here relates to "boy" cultural forms.

17 Harald E. L. Prins, "Visual Media and the Primitivist Perplex: Colonial Fantasies, Indigenous Imagination, and Advocacy in North America," in *Media Worlds: Anthropology on New Terrain*, eds. Faye D. Ginsburg, Lila Abu-Lughod, and Brian Larkin (Berkeley: University of California Press, 2002), 58.

18 Michel de Montaigne, "Of Cannibals," in *The Complete Essays of Montaigne,* trans. Donald M. Frame (Stanford, CA: Stanford University Press, 1958), 150–59.

19. Thomas Hobbes, "Leviathan," in *The Making of Society: An Outline of Sociology*, ed. Robert Bierstedt (New York: Modern Library, 1959), 88.

20 "Creativity" here is used in the sense explored by social theorist Hans Joas when describing "metaphors of creativity." See Hans Joas, *The Creativity of Action* (Chicago: University of Chicago Press, 1996). Joas examines four theories of creativity as developed by Herder ("Expression"), Marx ("Production" and "Revolution"), Schopenhauer and Nietzsche ("Life") and Dewey ("Intelligence and Reconstruction"). Joas emphasizes Dewey's pragmatism as "a theory of situated creativity" and as "emphasizing the aesthetic dimension of all human experience" (Joas, *Creativity of Action*, 133, 139), but I find it more appropriate to emphasize the productive element that he identifies in Marx's writings as the ground from which to strike a pragmatic stance vis-à-vis the intrapersonal nature of situated creativity. "Dewey stressed, as Hannah Arendt was later to do, that the basis of individuality was 'natality,' the very fact that a person had been born" (Joas, *Creativity of Action*, 140). Born into labor, but also born into creativity circumscribed by the circumstance of power.

21 John Dewey, *Experience and Education* (New York: Touchstone, 1997), 22.

22 For more on the notion of habitus, see Pierre Bourdieu and Loïc J. D. Wacquant, *An Invitation to Reflexive Sociology* (Chicago: University of Chicago, 1992), 18–19.

23 See for example Paolo Freire, *Pedagogy of the Oppressed* (New York: Continuum, 1998): "In contrast with the antidialogical and non-communicative 'deposits' of the banking method of education, the program content of the problem-posing method—dialogical par excellence—is constituted and organized by the students' view of the world, where their own generative themes are found. The content thus constantly expands and renews itself" (90). Freire's comment evokes the spirit of dialogue and problem-posing that I attempted to follow with my approach to producing *Trauber TV* with my students.

24 Other notable week-long series presented a Mariah Carey derived music video with backup singers and dancers mixing males and females all of whom were dressed in sexy outfits and a black-and-white series that featured recreations of Andy Kaufman routines from the Kaufman bio-pic *Man on the Moon* (1999).

25 Ellen Seiter, *Television and New Media Audiences* (New York: Oxford University Press, 1999), 89.

26 Donna J. Grace and Joseph Tobin, "Butt Jokes and Mean-Teacher Parodies: Video Production in the Elementary Classroom," in *Teaching Popular Culture: Beyond Radical Pedagogy*, ed. David Buckingham (London: University College London Press, 1998), 58.

27 In the wake of the Columbine shootings, repression and censorship was exactly the approach that many school administrators took in response to student challenges to school authority. Every deviant act, whether media-based or not, was seen as a warning sign of impending student violence. Of course, this harsh administrative response was itself inspired by the manner in which the media and the public excoriated school officials for not doing enough to prevent the Columbine incident. It seems that in the mind of the public-at-large students who consume and produce objectionable media should be subject to institutional repression regardless of the needs of academic freedom or open inquiry.

28 Barrie Thorne, *Gender Play: Girls and Boys in School* (New Brunswick, NJ: Rutgers University Press, 1993), 3.

29 Michel Foucault, *The History of Sexuality, Volume 1: An Introduction* (New York: Vintage, 1979), 93.

30 Pierre Bourdieu, *The Field of Cultural Production: Essays on Art and Literature* (New York: Columbia University Press, 1993), 65.

Chapter 5

1 Jerome S. Bruner, *The Process of Education* (Cambridge, MA: Harvard University Press, 1960), 84.

2 Orson Scott Card, *Ender's Game* (New York: Tom Doherty Associates, 1985).

3 From an interview with Richard Lindheim featured on the CBS Sunday Morning show, July 7, 2002.

4 This comes from a statement (circa 1999) quoted by Sharon Ghamari-Tabrizi in her essay, "The Convergence of the Pentagon and Hollywood: The Next Generation of Military Training Simulations," in *Memory Bytes: History, Technology, and Digital Culture*, eds. Lauren Rabinovitz and Abraham Geil (Durham, NC: Duke University Press, 2004), 165.

5 Lindheim's pronouncement sounds a peculiarly postmodern note. For example, his equating of the fictional, read simulation, for the real (a privileged site of bodily sensory coherence) strikes me as also evocative of the famous work of Jean Baudrillard and Fredric Jameson, not to mention that of *The Matrix* (which acknowledges its debt to Baudrillard's work). See Jean Baudrillard, "The Precession of the Simulacra," in *Simulacra and Simulation* (Ann Arbor: University of Michigan Press, 1994), 1–42; and Frederic Jameson, "Postmodernism and Consumer Society," in *The Cultural Turn: Selected Writings on the Postmodern, 1983–1998* (London: Verso, 1998), 1–20. Of course, much of postmodern high theory seems to draw inspiration from science fiction discourse as well.

6 Nicholas Garnham, *Emancipation, the Media, and Modernity: Arguments about the Media and Social Theory* (Oxford, UK: Oxford University Press, 2000), 70.

7 Allucquére Rosanne Stone, *The War of Desire and Technology at the Close of the Mechanical Age* (Cambridge, MA: MIT Press, 1995), 27.

8 STEVE stands for "Soar Training Expert for Virtual Environments." Throughout this chapter I will refer to this iteration of the ICT's pedagogical agent system as "Steve" to follow the conventions established by his designers.

9 Jeff Rickel, Jonathan Gratch, Randall Hill, Stacy Marsella, and William Swartout, "Steve Goes to Bosnia: Towards a New Generation of Virtual Humans for Interactive Experiences," *American Association for Artificial Intelligence*, (2001): 2–3.

10 Ibid., 1.

11 For the construct of politeness as a determining mode of human interaction in the ICT virtual humans, see Penelope Brown and Steven C. Levinson, *Politeness: Some Universals in Language Use* (Cambridge, UK: Cambridge University Press, 1987). For ideas related to the media equation, see Byron Reeves and Clifford Nass, *The Media Equation: How People Treat Computers, Television, and New Media Like Real People and Places* (Stanford, CA: Center for the Study of Language and Information, 1996).

12 Lewis Johnson, *Social Interactions with Agents* (Marina del Rey, CA: Center for Advanced Research in Technology for Education, Information Sciences Institute, University of Southern California, 2003).

13 Tom Gunning, "The Cinema of Attraction: Early Film, Its Spectator, and the Avant-Garde," in *Film and Theory: An Anthology*, eds. Robert Stam and Toby Miller (Malden, MA: Blackwell, 2000), 229–35.

14 In retrospect, my reading of the Sergeant-agent's expression as bewildered could be an example of one's need to read all actions as having emotional content. The agent could simply have been cycling through a series of "appropriate" responses to the query from Rasmussen.

15 Donna Haraway, "A Manifesto for Cyborgs: Science, Technology, and Socialist-Feminism in the Late Twentieth Century" in *The Haraway Reader* (New York: Routledge, 2003), 23.

16 Lev Manovich, *The Language of New Media* (Cambridge, MA: MIT Press, 2001), 57.

17 Phoebe Sengers, "Schizophrenia and Narrative in Artificial Agents," in *First Person: New Media as Story, Performance, and Game*, eds. Noah Wardrip-Fruin and Pat Harrigan (Cambridge, MA: MIT Press, 2006), 102.

18 See chapter 3, note 14 on the use of stereotypes in narrative construction with regard to *French in Action*.

19 An interesting note on the ethnicity of the African American sergeant who appears as the lead virtual human in the MRE simulation: I was told by Larry Rasmussen when I inquired about the choice of visual identity for the sergeant that it was merely coincidental as the most easily available model for the character animation designers was an African American colleague who was free for a photo session. The role that ethnic identity and notions of politeness and military command take when the African American face appears in MRE is interesting in

light of this casual approach taken toward the visuality and cultural construction of the virtual human agents.

20 For an exploration of the relationship between cognition and emotion and the ways in which these mental activities ground discussions on what qualities distinguish human from automaton, see Antonio Damasio, *Descartes' Error: Emotion, Reason, and the Human Brain* (New York: Penguin, 1994).

21 Richard S. Lazarus, "Emotions and Interpersonal Relationships: Toward a Person-centered Conceptualization of Emotions and Coping," *Journal of Personality* 74, no. 1 (2006): 14.

22 While sampling technologies have improved greatly—and will continue to improve as research continues on digital audio—there is still a qualitative difference that is discernible between analog and digital recordings. Obviously, sound quality differs from technology to technology—with many claiming that mp4 audio such as that on Apple's iTunes is wretched—but it remains true that sampled audio loses much of the tonal warmth of the original. For a nontechnical explanation related to audio and the digital image, see Herb Zettl's widely used production manual, *Video Basics*, 5th ed. (Belmont, CA: Thomson Wadsworth, 2007), 42–46.

23 Already in the time that has passed since I viewed the MRE and SASO-ST scenarios at the ICT, several more iterations of the virtual human simulations have been developed as evidenced by the website and YouTube channel for the institute. While the current crop of virtual humans circa 2012 are still a distance from attaining perfect worldly verisimilitude, the advances in character rendering and speech recognition are impressive. Search for keywords "Institute for Creative Technologies, University of Southern California" and navigate toward virtual human research on the links that appear in order to see the current versions of the ICT work in this area.

24 Lazarus, "Emotions and Interpersonal Relationships," 14.

25 For a lucid, perhaps even poetic, account of the cognitive science underlying Rasmussen's assertion, see the work of Antonio Damasio, in particular *Descartes' Error*, 141–49.

26 Alan Turing, "Computing Machinery and Intelligence," in *The New Media Reader*, eds. Noah Wardrip-Fruin and Nick Montfort (Cambridge, MA: MIT Press, 2003), 49–64.

27 Obviously, laden with a large dose of irony, DOCTOR's approach to therapy mirrors that found in many reductive versions of the therapeutic method attributed to psychologist Carl Rogers. For an emulation of the original DOCTOR program, see http://www-ai.ijs.si/eliza-cgi-bin/eliza_script.

28 Lucy A. Suchman, *Plans and Situated Actions: The Problem of Human–Machine Communication* (Cambridge, UK: Cambridge University Press, 1987), 23.

29 Reeves and Nass in their book *The Media Equation* provide considerable empirical evidence supporting this affective quality given to machines by their human users.

30 Jonathan Crary, *Techniques of the Observer: On Vision and Modernity in the Nineteenth Century* (Cambridge, MA: MIT Press, 1990), 147.

Conclusion

1 Marcel Proust, *Swann's Way*, trans. C. K. Scott Moncrieff, Terence Kilmartin, and D. J. Enright, Vol. 1, *In Search of Lost Time* (New York: Modern Library, 1998), 63–64.

2 Plato, *Phaedrus*, trans. W. C. Helmbold and W. G. Rabinowitz (New York: Macmillan, 1956), 68–69.

3 Obviously, Althusser's essay on the ideological function of state apparatuses—the school and the church—is the most famous statement critiquing the power of presence to shape the subject, but this idea, especially in relation to the church, has its roots in Luther and the Protestant Reformation. The simple insistence on reading the bible as a text stands as an important instance in the history of the book as subversive challenge to state authority embodied by the teacher. See Louis Althusser, "Ideology and Ideological State Apparatuses (Notes Towards an Investigation)," in *Mapping Ideology*, ed. Slavoj Zizek (London: Verso, 1994), 100–40; and

Elizabeth Eisenstein, *The Printing Revolution in Early Modern Europe* (Cambridge, UK: Cambridge University Press, 2005).

4 If one were to focus exclusively on the military applications of Steve and the ICT simulations, Virilio's book *War and Cinema* would be particularly illuminating, albeit burdened at times by a prophetic voice which often spins arguments into hyperbole. See Paul Virilio, *War and Cinema: The Logistics of Perception*, trans. Patrick Camiller (New York: Verso, 1988). In particular, Virilio's emphasis on the military agenda, during both the development of new technologies (with an eye to victory) and the military's use of human bodies as essentially cannon fodder for experimental science, speaks to issues that are resonant with some of the concerns examined in the ICT case study.

5 Paul Virilio, "The Third Interval: A Critical Transition," in *Rethinking Technologies*, ed. Verena A. Conley (Minneapolis: University of Minnesota Press, 1993), 10.

6 Friedrich A. Kittler, *Gramophone, Film, Typewriter* (Stanford, CA: Stanford University Press, 1999), 187.

7 The handwritten signature retains this relationship between authorship and the materiality of presence. With the increasing use of biometrics this sign of presence as inscription will most likely also disappear. During some credit transactions the cardholder's signature is represented by typing his or her name into a data field. This seems like the final move in Kittler's narrative of transforming presence through typography. Of course, biometrics (through scans, databases, and such) will most likely bring forth new forms of signature that will be intimately linked to identity and presence at a governmental, medical, and legal level.

8 Vivian Sobchack, "Toward a Phenomenology of Nonfictional Film Experience," in *Collecting Visible Evidence*, eds. Jane Gaines and Michael Renov (Minneapolis: University of Minnesota Press, 1999), 137.

9 Claude E. Shannon and Warren Weaver, *The Mathematical Theory of Communication* (Urbana: University of Illinois Press, 1949), 95–117.

10 Sherry Turkle, *Life on the Screen: Identity in the Age of the Internet* (New York: Simon & Shuster, 1995).

11 Ivan Illich, *Deschooling Society* (London: Marion Boyars, 2002), 17.

12 Paul Virilio, *Speed and Politics*, 2nd ed. (New York: Semiotext(e); Cambridge, MA: MIT Press, 2007).

13 Vilém Flusser, *Writings* (Minneapolis: University of Minnesota Press, 2002), 18.

14 John Durham Peters, *Speaking into the Air: A History of the Idea of Communication* (Chicago: University of Chicago Press, 1999), 33–62.

15 Hans Ulrich Gumbrecht, *Production of Presence: What Meaning Cannot Convey* (Stanford, CA: Stanford University Press, 2004), 130.

16 Diana Laurillard, *Rethinking University Teaching: A Conversational Framework for the Effective Use of Learning Technologies*, 2nd ed. (London: RoutledgeFalmer, 2002), 177.

17 Illich, *Deschooling Society*, 101.

18 Gumbrecht, *Production of Presence*, 131.

19 Raymond Williams, *Television: Technology and Cultural Form* (London: Routledge, 2003), 1–25.

20 Brian Winston, *Media Technology and Society: A History: From the Telegraph to the Internet* (London: Routledge, 1998), 1–18.

21 At this moment in time, contrary to the seemingly ever-present evangelists of educational technology, computers and new media technologies are not cost efficient methods for instruction. See for example from the dotcom boom era, Larry Cuban, *Oversold and Underused: Computers in the Classroom* (Cambridge, MA: Harvard University Press, 2001) and Todd Oppenheimer, "The Computer Delusion," *Atlantic Monthly* 280, no. 1 (1997): 45–62 and *The Flickering Mind: The False Promise of Technology in the Classroom and How Learning Can Be Saved* (New York: Random House, 2003). Considerable expenditures are required for installation, maintenance, and upgrade of any technological system. Also, note the increasingly popular attempts to use the iPad as the newly minted panacea for what ails education.

INDEX

Printed in the USA/Agawam, MA
January 31, 2013

572486.142